▶ **The Four Faces of the Republican Party**

DOI: 10.1057/9781137577535.0001

Other Palgrave Pivot titles

Indranarain Ramlall: **Central Bank Ratings: A New Methodology for Global Excellence**

Stephen Paul Miller: **The New Deal as a Triumph of Social Work: Frances Perkins and the Confluence of Early Twentieth Century Social Work with Mid-Twentieth Century Politics and Government**

Nicholas Pamment: **Community Reparation for Young Offenders: Perceptions, Policy and Practice**

David F. Tennant and Marlon R. Tracey: **Sovereign Debt and Credit Rating Bias**

Jefferson Walker: **King Returns to Washington: Explorations of Memory, Rhetoric, and Politics in the Martin Luther King, Jr. National Memorial**

Giovanni Barone Adesi and Nicola Carcano: **Modern Multi-Factor Analysis of Bond Portfolios: Critical Implications for Hedging and Investing**

Rilka Dragneva and Kataryna Wolczuk: **Ukraine between the EU and Russia: The Integration Challenge**

Viola Fabbrini, Massimo Guidolin and Manuela Pedio: **The Transmission Channels of Financial Shocks to Stock, Bond, and Asset-Backed Markets: An Empirical Analysis**

Timothy Wood: **Detainee Abuse During Op TELIC: 'A Few Rotten Apples'?**

Lars Klüver, Rasmus Øjvind Nielsen and Marie Louise Jørgensen (editors): **Policy-Oriented Technology Assessment Across Europe: Expanding Capacities**

Rebecca E. Lyons and Samantha J. Rayner (editors): **The Academic Book of the Future**

Ben Clements: **Surveying Christian Beliefs and Religious Debates in Post-War Britain**

Robert A. Stebbins: **Leisure and the Motive to Volunteer: Theories of Serious, Casual, and Project-Based Leisure**

Dietrich Orlow: **Socialist Reformers and the Collapse of the German Democratic Republic**

Gwendolyn Audrey Foster: **Disruptive Feminisms: Raced, Gendered, and Classed Bodies in Film**

Catherine A. Lugg: **US Public Schools and the Politics of Queer Erasure**

Olli Pyyhtinen: **More-than-Human Sociology: A New Sociological Imagination**

Jane Hemsley-Brown and Izhar Oplatka: **Higher Education Consumer Choice**

Arthur Asa Berger: **Gizmos or: The Electronic Imperative: How Digital Devices have Transformed American Character and Culture**

Antoine Vauchez: **Democratizing Europe**

DOI: 10.1057/9781137577535.0001

THE FOUR FACES OF THE REPUBLICAN

on   Good

on   Walden   Aisle N   Bay 12 Item 9396

ption   May have some shelf-wear due to normal use. Your
            purchase funds free job training and education in the
            greater Seattle area. Thank you for supporting
            Goodwill's nonprofit mission!

            Prescanned

            0KVOFY00B7ZM

            1137577487

            9781137577481

ode

mployee   1ngvillarpando

Date Added 4/14/2023 1:43:14 PM

THE FOUR FATES OF THE REPUBLICAN

palgrave▸pivot

The Four Faces of the Republican Party: The Fight for the 2016 Presidential Nomination

Henry Olsen

and

Dante J. Scala

palgrave
macmillan

DOI: 10.1057/9781137577535.0001

First published 2016 by
PALGRAVE MACMILLAN

The authors have asserted their rights to be identified as the authors of this work in accordance with the Copyright, Designs and Patents Act 1988.

Palgrave Macmillan in the UK is an imprint of Macmillan Publishers Limited, registered in England, company number 785998, of Houndmills, Basingstoke, Hampshire RG21 6XS.

Palgrave Macmillan in the US is a division of Nature America, Inc., One New York Plaza, Suite 4500 New York, NY 10004-1562.

Palgrave Macmillan is the global academic imprint of the above companies and has companies and representatives throughout the world.

Hardback ISBN: 978-1-137-57748-1
E-PUB ISBN: 978-1-137-57752-8
E-PDF ISBN: 978-1-137-5773-5
DOI: 10.1057/9781137577535

Distribution in the UK, Europe and the rest of the world is by Palgrave Macmillan®, a division of Macmillan Publishers Limited, registered in England, company number 785998, of Houndmills, Basingstoke, Hampshire RG21 6XS.

Library of Congress Cataloging-in-Publication Data is available from the Library of Congress

A catalog record for this book is available from the Library of Congress

A catalogue record for the book is available from the British Library

For my parents, Henry and Dorothy Olsen, and for my first political mentors and teachers, Robert L. Walker, Jr., Alan Heslop, and Allan Hoffenblum – Henry Olsen

For Julie – Dante J. Scala

DOI: 10.1057/9781137577535.0001

Contents

List of Figures — vii

List of Tables — ix

Personal Acknowledgments — xi

Professional Acknowledgments — xii

1 Republican Presidential Politics — 1

2 Moderate and Liberal Republican Primary Voters — 33

3 Somewhat Conservatives — 60

4 Very Conservative Evangelicals — 80

5 Very Conservative Seculars — 104

6 The Paths to the 2016 Republican Nomination — 122

Bibliography — 148

Index — 157

DOI: 10.1057/9781137577535.0001

List of Figures

2.1 Presence of moderates and liberals in
     Republican primaries and caucuses   36
2.2 John McCain's performance among moderates
     and liberals, 2000   43
2.3 Preference for Republican nomination,
     December 2007   47
2.4 McCain's relative performance among
     moderates and liberals, 2008   51
2.5 Mitt Romney's relative performance among
     moderates and liberals, 2012   55
3.1 Presence of somewhat conservative voters in
     Republican primaries and caucuses   63
3.2 George W. Bush's relative performance among
     somewhat conservative voters, 2000   68
3.3 McCain's relative performance among
     somewhat conservative voters, 2008   71
3.4 Romney's relative performance among
     somewhat conservative voters, 2012   77
4.1 Presence of very conservative evangelicals in
     Republican primaries and caucuses   84
4.2 Bush's relative performance among very
     conservative evangelicals, 2000   90
4.3 Mike Huckabee's relative performance among
     very conservative evangelicals, 2008   96
4.4 Rick Santorum's relative performance among
     very conservative evangelicals, 2012   98
5.1 Presence of very conservative secular voters in
     Republican primaries and caucuses   106

5.2   Bush's relative performance among very conservative
      seculars, 2000   114
5.3   Romney's performance among very conservative
      seculars, 2008   116
6.1   Composition of Republican electorates in first four
      contests of 2016   127
6.2   Composition of Republican electorates in March 1
      primaries, 2016   131
6.3   Composition of Republican electorates in later
      March primaries, 2016   131
6.4   Composition of Republican electorates after April 1, 2016   132

DOI: 10.1057/9781137577535.0002

List of Tables

2.1 Profile of moderate and liberal Republican voters   38

2.2 Candidate performance among moderate and liberal voters, 2000   44

2.3 Logistic regression analysis of McCain's vote in 2000, post-South Carolina   45

2.4 Candidate performance among moderate and liberal voters, 2008   52

2.5 Logistic regression of McCain vote in 2008, post-South Carolina   53

2.6 Candidate performance among moderate and liberal voters, 2012   56

2.7 Logistic regression of Romney vote in 2012, post-Florida   57

3.1 Profile of somewhat conservative Republican voters   64

3.2 Candidate performance among somewhat conservative voters, 2000   69

3.3 Candidate performance among somewhat conservative voters, 2008   72

3.4 Candidate performance among somewhat conservative voters, 2012   77

4.1 Profile of very conservative evangelical voters   83

4.2 Candidate performance among very conservative evangelicals, 2000   90

4.3 Logistic regression of Bush vote in 2000, post-South Carolina   91

4.4 Candidate performance among very conservative evangelicals, 2008   94

4.5   Logistic regression of Huckabee vote in 2008,
      post-South Carolina   97
4.6   Candidate performance among very conservative
      evangelicals, 2012   100
4.7   Logistic regression of Gingrich primary vote in 2012,
      post-Florida   101
4.8   Logistic regression of Santorum primary vote in 2012,
      post-Florida   102
5.1   Profile of very conservative secular voters   108
5.2   Candidate performance among very conservative
      secular voters, 2000   114
5.3   Candidate performance among very conservative
      seculars, 2008   117
5.4   Candidate performance among very conservative
      seculars, 2012   119

DOI: 10.1057/9781137577535.0003

Personal Acknowledgments

Our thanks to Daniel Bromberg, Alan Gitelson, Caitlin Jewett, Barbara Norrander, Arthur Paulson, Andrew Smith, Wayne Steger, and an anonymous reader for their sage advice on this project at various stages. We extend special gratitude to Edward Plank. Adam Kelly and Michael Branley provided important early research assistance. The University of New Hampshire provided research support throughout our work. At Palgrave Macmillan, Brian O'Connor took initial interest in our project. Alexandra Dauler and Elaine Fan steadily guided it to completion. Any errors or omissions remaining are the responsibility of the authors.

Professional Acknowledgments

The authors thank the editors of *The National Interest* for their permission in using material first published in their magazine in March–April 2014. In addition, the authors acknowledge the Roper Center for Public Opinion Research for their assistance in procuring the polling data used in their research.

▶

DOI: 10.1057/9781137577535.0005

1

Republican Presidential Politics

Abstract: *This chapter lays out the outline of the book, an analysis of the Republican presidential primary electorate, and reviews the literature on presidential nomination campaigns. Using primary exit poll data, the authors will profile four factions of the Republican Party: moderates and liberals; somewhat conservative voters; very conservative evangelicals; and very conservative secular voters. Scholars typically focus on momentum and elite influence as key factors in determining the nomination. The authors argue that it is also important to understand the factions of a political party and their interactions. Candidates first aim to become champions of one or more factions, and then attempt to build coalitions with other factions in the later stages of the nomination process.*

Keywords: presidential elections; presidential primaries; Republican Party

Olsen, Henry, and Dante J. Scala. *The Four Faces of the Republican Party: The Fight for the 2016 Presidential Nomination.* New York: Palgrave Macmillan, 2016. DOI: 10.1057/9781137577535.0006.

The common wisdom holds that the contest for the 2016 Republican presidential nomination will boil down to a joust between the "establishment" and the "insurgents." The former will allegedly be more moderate and the latter more conservative. Since most polls for two decades have shown that around two-thirds to 70 percent of self-described Republicans call themselves conservative, this elite narrative will focus on just how much the establishment candidate will need to be pulled to the right in order to fend off his insurgent challenger. And since the Tea Party has clearly become a vocal and powerful insurgent element in the GOP, the narrative will focus on two other questions: Who will gain Tea Party favor and emerge as the insurgent candidate? And can the establishment candidate escape becoming Tea Partyized during the primary season and therefore remain a viable general-election candidate?

The common wisdom has the advantage of being a neat, coherent, and exciting story. It also allows political journalists to do what they like to do most, which is to focus on the personalities of the candidates and the tactics they employ. It has only one small problem. It is wrong.

Exit and entrance polls of Republican primaries and caucuses going back to 2000 show that the Republican presidential electorate is remarkably stable. It does not divide neatly along establishment-versus-conservative lines. Rather, the GOP contains four discrete factions that are based primarily on ideology, with elements of class and religious background tempering that focus. Open nomination contests during this period are resolved first by how candidates become favorites of each of these factions, and then by how they are positioned to absorb the voting blocs of the other factions as their favorites drop out. Over the following pages, we will discuss how these factions of the Republican Party

- ▶ consistently desire different qualities in a nominee, and are drawn to candidates who best display those qualities;
- ▶ regularly voice different policy priorities that they wish their nominee to pursue first and foremost;
- ▶ line up behind certain candidates as their champions, based on their qualities, policy priorities, and perceived viability to gain the nomination; and
- ▶ persist in their support of their champions until they drop out of the race, then move toward second-best options in the remaining field if their favorites depart.

DOI: 10.1057/9781137577535.0006

This analysis allows us to explain what we consistently observe. It explains why a conservative party rarely nominates the most conservative candidate. It explains why the party often seems to nominate the "next in line." And, perhaps most importantly, it explains why certain candidates emerge as the "surprise" candidate in each race. Analysts and advisers who understand this elemental map of the Republican electorate will be better positioned to navigate the shoals of the nominating river and bring their favored candidate safely home to port.

Republican voters fall into four rough camps. They are: moderate or liberal voters; somewhat conservative voters; very conservative, evangelical voters; and very conservative, secular voters. Each of these groups supports extremely different types of candidates. Each of these groups has also demonstrated stable preferences over the past 15 years. Using exit-poll data from the 2000, 2008, and 2012 Republican presidential primaries, we will present a profile of each of these party factions.[1] The Republican presidential primaries in 2000, 2008, and 2012 are an excellent opportunity to study the Republican primary electorate without confounding factors. All of these contests were free-for-alls, without an incumbent president or vice president who would be expected to win the nomination of his party easily (Mayer 2010), as George W. Bush did in 2004. In 2008, Vice President Dick Cheney declined to run for president, leaving the contest open to numerous contenders. The last three Republican contests allow us to observe how the various factions of the party electorate reacted toward various candidates as they attempt to build coalitions that would deliver them their party's nomination.

Moderate and liberal Republicans

The bloc of moderates and liberal voters is surprisingly strong in Republican presidential primaries and caucuses, comprising the second-largest voting bloc with approximately 25–30 percent of all GOP voters nationwide. They are especially strong in early voting states such as New Hampshire (where they have comprised between 45 and 49 percent of the GOP electorate between 1996 and 2012), Florida, and Michigan. They are, however, surprisingly numerous even in the Deep South, the most conservative portion of the country. Moderates or liberals have comprised between 31 and 39 percent of the South Carolina electorate

DOI: 10.1057/9781137577535.0006

since 1996, outnumbering or roughly equaling very conservative voters in each of those years.

Moderate and liberal voters prefer someone who is both more secular and less fiscally conservative than their somewhat conservative cousins. In 1996, for example, they preferred Tennessee senator Lamar Alexander over Bob Dole. In 2000, they were the original McCainiacs, supporting a candidate who backed campaign-finance regulation, opposed tax cuts for the top bracket, and criticized the influence of Pat Robertson. In 2008, they stuck with John McCain, giving him their crucial backing in New Hampshire and providing his margin of victory in virtually every state. In 2012, they began firmly in Ron Paul's or Jon Huntsman's camp. Paul and Huntsman together won 43 percent of their vote in Iowa and 50 percent in New Hampshire. Once it became clear that their candidates could not win, however, the moderate-liberal faction swung firmly toward former Massachusetts governor Mitt Romney in his fights with former Speaker of the House Newt Gingrich and former Pennsylvania Senator Rick Santorum.

This latter movement is perhaps most indicative of their true preferences. The moderate or liberal voter seems motivated by a candidate's secularism above all else. They will always vote for the Republican candidate who seems least overtly religious and are motivated to oppose the candidate who is most overtly religious. This makes them a secure bank of votes for a somewhat conservative candidate who emerges from the early stages of the primary season in a battle with a religious conservative, as occurred in 1996, 2008, and 2012.

"Somewhat conservative" Republicans

The most important of these groups is the one most journalists do not understand and therefore ignore: the somewhat conservative voters. This group is the most numerous nationally and in many states, comprising 35–40 percent of the national GOP electorate. While the numbers of liberal and moderate, very conservative, and evangelical voters vary significantly by state, somewhat conservative voters are found in similar proportions in every state. They are not very vocal, but they form the bedrock base of the Republican Party.

They also have a significant distinction: they always back the winner. The candidate who garners their favor has won each of the last four open

DOI: 10.1057/9781137577535.0006

races. This tendency runs down to the state level as well. Look at the exit polls from virtually any state caucus or primary since 1996 and you will find that the winner either received a plurality, or ran roughly even, among the somewhat conservative voters.

These voters' preferred candidate profile can be inferred from the characteristics of their favored candidates: Bob Dole in 1996, Bush in 2000, McCain in 2008, and Romney in 2012. They like even-keeled men with substantial governing experience. They like people who express conservative values on the economy or social issues, but who do not espouse radical change. They like people who are optimistic about America; the somewhat conservative voter rejects the "culture warrior" motif that characterized Pat Buchanan's campaigns. They are conservative in both senses of the word; they prefer the ideals of American conservatism while displaying the cautious disposition of the Burkean.

Very conservative evangelicals

The third-largest group is the moderates' bête noire: the very conservative evangelicals. This group is small compared to the others, comprising around one-fifth of all GOP voters. They gain significant strength, however, from three unique factors. First, they are geographically concentrated in Southern and border states, where they can comprise a quarter or more of a state's electorate. Moreover, somewhat conservative voters in Southern and border states are also likelier to be evangelical, and they tend to vote for more socially conservative candidates than do their non-Southern, nonevangelical ideological cousins. Finally, they are very motivated to turn out in caucus states, such as Iowa and Kansas, and form the single largest bloc of voters in those races.

These factors have given very conservative, evangelical-backed candidates unusual strength in Republican presidential contests. The evangelical favorite, for example, surprised pundits by winning Iowa in 2008 and 2012, and supplied the backing for second-place Iowa finishers Pat Robertson in 1988 and Pat Buchanan in 1996. Their strength in the Deep South and the border states also allowed Mike Huckabee rather than Romney to emerge as McCain's final challenger in 2008, and that strength combined with their domination of the February 7 caucuses in Minnesota and Colorado allowed Santorum to emerge as Romney's challenger in 2012.

DOI: 10.1057/9781137577535.0006

This group prefers candidates who are very open about their religious beliefs, place a high priority on social issues such as gay marriage and abortion, and see the United States in decline because of its movement away from the faith and moral codes of its past. Their favored candidates tend to be economically more open to government intervention. Santorum, for example, advocated policies friendly to manufacturing, and Buchanan opposed the North American Free Trade Agreement in the 1990s. This social conservatism and economic moderation tends to place these candidates out of line with the center of the Republican Party, the somewhat conservative voter outside the Deep South. Each evangelical-backed candidate has lost this group decisively in primaries in the Midwest, Northeast, Pacific Coast, and mountain states. Indeed, they even lose them in Southern-tinged states like Virginia and Texas, where McCain's ability to win the somewhat conservative voters, coupled with huge margins among moderates and liberals, allowed him to hold off Huckabee in one-on-one face-offs in 2008.

Very conservative, secular voters

The final and smallest GOP tribe is the one that Washington D.C. elites are most familiar with: the very conservative, secular voters. This group comprises a tiny 5–10 percent nationwide and thus never sees its choice emerge from the initial races to contend in later stages. Jack Kemp and Pete DuPont in 1988; Steve Forbes or Phil Gramm in 1996 and 2000; Fred Thompson or Romney in 2008; Herman Cain, Rick Perry, or Gingrich in 2012: each of these candidates showed promise in early polling but foundered in early races once voters became more familiar with each of the candidates. Secular moderates and somewhat conservative voters preferred candidates with less materialistic, sweeping economic radicalism while very conservative evangelicals went with someone singing from their hymnal. Thus, these voters quickly had to choose which of the remaining candidates to support in subsequent races.

This small but influential bloc likes urbane, fiscally oriented men. Thus, they preferred Kemp or DuPont in 1988, Forbes or Gramm in 1996, Forbes in 2000, and Romney in 2008. In 2012, this group was tempted by Perry until his lack of sophistication became painfully obvious in the early debates. It then flirted with Gingrich until his temperamental issues

DOI: 10.1057/9781137577535.0006

resurfaced in Florida. After that, faced with the choice of Santorum or Romney, it swung behind Romney en masse.

The latter example is in fact this group's modus operandi. They invariably see their preferred candidate knocked out early, and they then invariably back whoever is supported by the somewhat conservative bloc. Forbes's early exit from the 2000 race, for example, was crucial to Bush's ability to win South Carolina against the McCain onslaught. In New Hampshire, Bush won only 33 percent of the very conservative vote; Forbes received 20 percent. With Forbes out of the race, however, Bush was able to capture 74 percent of the very conservative vote in South Carolina.

The 2016 primaries and caucuses: champion your faction, build your coalition

The road to the Republican nomination formally begins with the Iowa caucuses and the New Hampshire primary. Candidates for the presidential nomination of their party (as well as the media that cover them) regard these first-in-the-nation states as the dispenser of that magical elixir known as "momentum." In the frantic process of "winnowing," pundits often draw a cause-and-effect relationship between a candidate's ability to exceed the expectations of conventional media wisdom, and his potential to convert performance in these first two contests into success in subsequent primaries. Excessive focus on the media-expectations game leads to a narrow reading of the vote totals, with a lack of serious thought about what those votes represent in terms of core party constituencies. Shifting the focus to the "core fundamentals" of a candidate's performance—that is, how the candidate performed among the core Republican constituencies we have described earlier—offers a perspective that tempers the exuberance regarding the significance of strong candidate performance in the early states. Concentrating on core fundamentals of a candidate's support also puts perspective on the effects of media perception on a candidate's performance.

In this chapter, we develop the concept of early primaries and caucuses as "knockout rounds." These first contests in the process not only bestow momentum. They also crown the champions of the various factions within the Republican Party. Santorum and Huckabee, for example, did not benefit from winning Iowa simply because they outperformed media

DOI: 10.1057/9781137577535.0006

expectations. They also benefited because they won Iowa by successfully courting conservative evangelicals—and thus became the national champion of that faction the day after Iowa. In similar fashion, McCain and Romney gained from winning New Hampshire by earning the allegiance of moderate and liberal Republicans seeking a champion.

After the knockout rounds, surviving candidates seek to build a coalition of voters from other factions. The task of coalition-building helps to explain why, in a party widely assumed to be moving rightward, candidates championing the moderate faction of the party (such as McCain in 2008, and Romney in 2012) have been more successful in building coalitions than their more conservative competitors for the nomination. Tea Party candidates, in contrast, face the following dilemma: They either must deny any breathing space to a more evangelical candidate, or they must emulate Bush in 2000 in having enough appeal to other factions. The likelier outcome is a repeat of the traditional GOP three-way war between its somewhat conservative center and the two large ideological wings: the moderate secularists and conservative evangelicals.

Past need not be prologue, however. In the movie *Lawrence of Arabia*, Peter O'Toole's Lawrence decides to go back into a hellish desert to rescue a straggler. His close aide, Sherif Ali, tells him not to bother, that the straggler's fate is foreordained. "It is written," Ali tells the Englishman. "Nothing is written," Lawrence angrily yells back. He then goes into the desert and returns with his man. Lawrence could conquer the desert and its heat through his will, but he could not will the desert away. GOP aspirants would do well to emulate Lawrence's will and resourcefulness, but they too cannot will away their surroundings. Whichever candidate from whatever faction emerges, he or she will have done so by understanding the four species of GOP voters and using their wiles and the calendar to their advantage. For truly, as Ali said of Lawrence, for some men nothing is written until they write it.

The political science of presidential primaries

Our study draws upon four decades' worth of scholarship on the modern presidential nomination process. Those wishing to learn more about the political science of presidential nominations, and how we see our work contributing to that body of knowledge, will find the following pages of interest. Those

DOI: 10.1057/9781137577535.0006

primarily interested in our analysis of exit-poll data may skim the following section, or bookmark it for future reference, and move on to Chapter 2.

The modern presidential nomination process began in 1972, after Democratic Party reforms ended a process in which state and local party bosses decided who their standard bearer would be in the November general election. In the new, more democratic system, candidates now had to build national campaigns in order to accumulate a majority of convention delegates in a series of caucuses and primaries. Surprises occurred immediately: liberal South Dakota Senator George McGovern upset frontrunner Maine Senator Ed Muskie to become the Democratic nominee in 1972. Four years later, former California governor Ronald Reagan nearly defeated sitting President Gerald Ford for the Republican nomination, and little-known Georgia governor Jimmy Carter emerged from the primaries as the Democratic nominee. To explain Carter's surprise success, political scientists devised the dynamic of "momentum" (for a classic treatment of the subject, see Bartels [1988]). Candidates such as Carter capture momentum during the nomination season by winning early contests such as the Iowa caucuses and the New Hampshire primary, thus gaining media attention, stature among voters, and additional sources of campaign funding.

Carter's success, however, proved difficult to duplicate. Colorado Senator Gary Hart, for example, gained early momentum in 1984 but former Vice President Walter Mondale ultimately became the Democratic nominee. Buchanan upset Dole in the 1996 New Hampshire primary, but Dole nonetheless proceeded to capture the Republican nomination. As frontrunners for the nomination became more difficult to dislodge, political scientists began to reconsider the importance of momentum. Some argued that momentum was overrated because the most important events in the nomination process occurred before caucuses and elections began. During this "invisible primary" period, party elites sought to reach consensus on a nominee. When they succeeded (and they often did), primary voters merely ratified the decision of elites.

We agree that candidate momentum and elite approval both play important roles in the presidential nomination process of the Republican Party, but argue that both explanations tend to underplay the role of party factions in determining the nominee. Momentum, we concur with Popkin (1994), is essentially the rapid public exposure of a candidate to the entire nation following a victory in an early contest (also see Dutwin [2000]). Early contests also provide new information about expected candidate performance to voters who participate in later contests, and thus allows them to act strategically and avoid wasting their votes on candidates likely to fail. Our close examination of primary exit polls shows that once early momentum establishes which candidate becomes the favorite (or the nemesis) of a particular faction, that candidate's share of the vote within each faction becomes relatively fixed and changes only because of demographic differences among states and the departure of other candidates from the race. Elite approval matters a great deal—not just because of the importance of elites, but because those elites tend to have the same viewpoints and preferences as the largest Republican voting bloc. When a candidate possesses money and elite approval but does not share those voters' values, as John Connally did in 1980 and Rudy Giuliani did in 2008, no amount of elite approval and cash on hand can rescue that campaign from certain defeat.

Momentum and attrition

The momentum model focuses on primary and caucus voters, who make decisions that determine the nominees during the year of the presidential election (Norrander 1993). Momentum has been compared to "the miracle of compound interest": Early victories (or better than expected performances) enable a candidate to acquire more resources to spend on upcoming primaries, thus improving their chances for further victories (Aldrich 1980). Success in a primary also generates increased positive media, a significant factor given the fact that the nomination is determined in a sequence of events. The media set public perceptions, for instance, on whether a second-place finish exceeds expectations or fails to meet expectations. One such turning point in media expectations is the first voting in the Iowa caucuses. Buchanan won just 22,000 votes in the 1996 Iowa caucuses, but his second-place finish was depicted as a surprise, and his mentions in the press grew substantially immediately afterward. Huckabee enjoyed a similar boost in media attention after his Iowa victory in 2008. The boost in media attention for an unexpectedly strong performance may then aid the candidate in the next contest in New Hampshire. This is why "long-shot" candidates traditionally spend their resources in early contests in an attempt to acquire momentum by performing surprisingly well (Gurian 1986; Gurian and Haynes 1993; for more on candidates' primary spending strategies, see Gurian [1993a,

DOI: 10.1057/9781137577535.0006

b]). A survey of voters in 2008 "Super Tuesday" primaries indicates that the results of Iowa and New Hampshire affect how voters in these later states perceive candidates' viability and electability (Redlawsk et al. 2011). Armed with greater name recognition and monetary resources, the candidate with momentum is primed to improve performance in subsequent contests.

How do media reports affect primary voters who participate in the nomination contest after Iowa and New Hampshire? Political scientists have devised a host of explanations. Voters are susceptible to "contagion," that is, candidates with momentum attract the perhaps irrational exuberance of voters who offer their support in the immediate aftermath of victory. In addition, there are voters who desire the self-satisfaction of supporting a winner. Other voters back a candidate with momentum because they regard momentum as proof of electability, the ability to perform strongly as the party's nominee in the general election. Some primary voters, seeking a short cut for making their decisions, follow the cues of fellow partisans from previous primaries and back the candidate with momentum. Still others surrender their will to the seemingly inevitable nominee (Bartels 1988; Kenney and Rice 1994). Voters may behave strategically, choosing a candidate they like second-best because they believe his candidacy is more viable, or likely to win the nomination, than their favorite's campaign. Still other voters in later primaries may not have committed to a particular candidate, and thus are quite malleable to candidate momentum. When voters in later primaries and caucuses perceive that a candidate has gained popular support, this perception affects their attitudes toward the candidate, which may in turn change their vote choice. Specifically, voters hear of others' views of a candidate, consider their rationales for those views, and in so doing are persuaded more favorably toward that candidate. In this way, candidate momentum could be especially effective among people who do not have strong commitments to a candidate. During presidential nomination contests, the media offers continual updates on how candidates are faring. Given the months-long process, primary voters have considerable time to absorb this information. And while these voters gain knowledge about the pros and cons of various potential nominees, many do not have strong commitments to a candidate. The voters most susceptible to momentum are "the less-involved segment of a highly involved group." While groups of voters with high levels of political awareness might be more likely to counterargue and resist persuasion, those with just a moderate level of involvement are more persuadable by "consensus cues." People do not simply climb on the bandwagon without thinking, but they do reconsider their own opinions in response to the views of others around them (Mutz 1997).

Candidate momentum appears overpowering in the flush of victory, but recedes over time. Recent Republican primary cycles have illustrated Norrander's (2006) point that "momentum is often short lived." Candidates touted as possessing momentum often nonetheless falter, ultimately finishing as the runner-up to the eventual nominee. McCain in 2000, Huckabee in 2008, and Santorum in 2012 are all examples of the limitations of momentum in the nomination process (for a study of momentum in the 2012 nomination process, see McGowen and Palazzolo [2014]). Republican primary voters nationwide learn about the candidates who emerge from Iowa, New Hampshire, or South Carolina, but momentum is not necessarily enough to convince them to jump on board. As we will show, all three candidates increased their overall support after their early victories, but they did so primarily on their increased strength within one faction of the Republican Party. In the early stages of 2016, candidates will compete in the four "carve out" states whose place at the front of the calendar is protected by the national political parties: Iowa, New Hampshire, Nevada, and South Carolina. Once the first four contests of the nomination cycle conclude, each candidate hopes to become the first choice of one of the factions. The first four contests are crucial because the national media publicity gives the winners tens of millions of dollars in free media coverage, effectively sending their message in a favorable light to the entire nation. As a result, in 2000 moderate Republican voters in Ohio or Massachusetts followed the lead of their counterparts in New Hampshire and voted for McCain. In 2008, Southern conservative evangelicals recognized that their fellow believers in Iowa had, in effect, crowned a champion for their faction of the party and backed Huckabee. These candidates' momentum, however, faltered at the edge of their respective factions.

The other dynamic in play during the sequence of primaries and caucuses is attrition. Every field of candidates, no matter how large, narrows down quickly to two or three with a plausible chance of winning the nomination. Norrander (2000, 2006) describes the nomination season not in terms of momentum, but as an "attrition game," inasmuch as the departure of candidates from the race shapes the endgame of the process. In terms of their ability to survive the attrition game, three types of presidential nomination campaigns exist.

The first type of campaign spends a great deal of resources and is built to last a long time. Nominees typically emerge from this type of campaign. The second type of campaign spends small amounts of resources, but nonetheless tends to persist to the latter stages of the nomination season. These campaigns feature non-traditional candidates such as Buchanan or Alan Keyes (or on the Democratic side, Jesse Jackson) who raise little money but nonetheless remain in business with low-cost campaigning. Some of these candidates survive by filling an "electoral niche" within the field of candidates (Steger et al. 2002). They aim to appeal to a portion of the party. These candidates tend to be policy advocates, those whose first priority is not necessarily to win the nomination, but rather to influence the party agenda. These candidates also tend to draw from one particular party faction, in terms of voters and contributors; as a result, they do not require the financial resources required for those intent on winning the office. While mainstream candidates prioritize fundraising and their competitiveness with the frontrunner in determining when to exit, policy seekers focus on whether they are receiving media coverage. Such coverage aids in increasing fundraising, which in turn allows these long-shots to compete in primaries. A prime example of this type of candidate was Santorum in 2012. A late burst in the polls days before the Iowa caucuses led to a flurry of free media coverage. Santorum's narrow victory in Iowa, in turn, was the catalyst for donor support that enabled him to become one of Romney's main challengers for the nomination and remain in the race beyond expectations.

A third group falls in the middle: traditional candidates who have failed to reach the top tier of campaigns in terms of money and standing in national public opinion polls (Norrander 2006). These are the candidates whose future depends most on early victories in Iowa and New Hampshire and subsequent momentum for later contests. Most abandon their attempts because their campaigns lack the resilience of the front runners. It is easier to survive in the first states, because campaign resources are "relatively elastic" in the early stages (Steger et al. 2002). Resourceful candidates find ways to do more with less. Pat Robertson, for example, substituted the work of grassroots volunteers for paid staff; Buchanan was masterful at attracting free media to substitute for paid media such as television advertising. But these resources become "increasingly inelastic and nonsubstitutable" in the later stages of the

DOI: 10.1057/9781137577535.0006

race, causing resource scarcity and disparity at the same time they are more in demand. In addition, the media are quick to dismiss early losers as failed candidates, and turn off the spout of free media. As a result, primaries and caucuses tend to winnow the field over time.

The key to the nomination, Norrander (2006) stresses, is not momentum, but survival: Candidates win the nomination these days by following Romney's method: dominating the process before caucuses and primaries actually begin, and then ensuring enough popular support in Iowa and New Hampshire "to avoid being winnowed from the field" (for more on attrition, see Haynes et al. [2004]).

Elite influence and the invisible primary

As the new system of nominating presidential candidates matured in the 1980s and 1990s, political scientists began to reconsider exactly how democratic the nomination process had become. Certainly, a considerable amount of power had been bestowed upon ordinary, rank-and-file party members who had the opportunity to participate in caucuses and primaries. Did this mean, however, that party elites had surrendered their traditional authority over the outcome? Perhaps these elites had adjusted to the changes in the rules, and now reasserted their influence over the nomination process in other ways. To explore this possibility, scholars began to focus on what occurred before the first primaries and caucuses were held—the "invisible primary," as journalist Arthur Hadley (1976) called it—which took place between the end of the last presidential election season and the beginning of the next cycle's primaries and caucuses. During the invisible primary, candidates build their national campaigns, and vie for the support of political, moneyed, and media elites. If elites no longer enjoy the luxury of sitting in a smoke-filled room and directly deciding the nominee of their party, they can still strongly influence who emerges on the short list of plausible nominees during a time that most voters are paying scant attention.

In the 1990s, political scientist William Mayer (1996) built a forecasting model intended to quantify the effects of the invisible primary on the outcome of the nomination process. Mayer's model consciously ignored any effects of early-contest momentum, and instead focused on just two factors that were established before the primaries and caucuses began: the candidate's standing in national polls immediately prior to the

DOI: 10.1057/9781137577535.0006

beginning of primary and caucus season; and the monetary resources the candidate accumulated during the invisible primary. Mayer's model had early success predicting nomination outcomes, and other scholars followed his lead (most notably, Adkins and Dowdle [2000 and 2001] which added New Hampshire primary results and Iowa caucus results to the forecasting model; Steger et al. [2004] on the New Hampshire effect; and Adkins and Dowdle [2005]. On the effects of Iowa and New Hampshire during the invisible primary, see Christenson and Smidt [2012]; Smith and Scala [2007-08]).

Wealthy elites' ability to influence which candidates have the resources to run a national campaign has only increased over time. By leaps and bounds, presidential campaigns have become increasingly expensive, far outstripping the public financing system's capacity to even the playing field by partially matching donors' contributions. (Bill Clinton was the last president to accept public matching funds. Nowadays, serious candidates forego matching funds in order to ignore the spending cap, and make unlimited expenditures in primaries and caucuses.) For instance, by the end of March 2012, the Romney campaign had spent more than $75 million securing the nomination.[2] Elites often build fundraising networks, using a process known as "bundling." One of the key obstacles of raising campaign money is that a donor could only make a maximum contribution of $1,000 (until it was doubled to $2,000 by the Bipartisan Campaign Reform Act of 2002 and indexed to inflation; the maximum amount a donor can give now is $2,700). Raising millions of dollars $1,000 at a time was quite consuming for the candidate. In 2000, Bush's campaign decided to delegate this burdensome task. The candidate tapped members of his extensive political network and asked them not only to donate money, but also to ask members of their business and social networks to contribute as well. Once volunteers collected these donations, they would be "bundled" together and sent to the campaign. (In return, these volunteers might be rewarded with perks such as meetings with the candidate.) All told, more than 200 bundlers, titled "Pioneers," each put together at least $100,000 in funds for the Bush campaign, for a total of more than $22 million. Other successful candidates adopted this technique in subsequent elections, such as John Kerry, McCain, and Barack Obama, who raised more than $60 million in 2008 thanks to the help of bundlers (Hasen 2009). The increasing cost of presidential campaigns has created a divide between haves and have-nots;

DOI: 10.1057/9781137577535.0006

"the playing field is effectively tilted in favor of those obtaining money, media exposure, and partisan support" (Steger 2008b; see also Adkins and Dowdle 2002; Steger et al. 2004).

The newest invention in presidential campaign financing is the "super PAC," or independent expenditure-only committee. In just three election cycles, super PACs have become vehicles for the raising and spending of hundreds of millions of dollars for political campaigns, after a pair of 2010 decisions by the federal courts, *Citizens United* v. *Federal Election Commission* and *SpeechNOW.org* v. *Federal Election Commission*. There are no limits on how much money a person may donate to a super PAC. As a result, just one wealthy donor can ensure that a super PAC has enough money to operate throughout the presidential nomination season. The federal courts removed caps on donors' contributions under the condition that super PACs would only make independent expenditures, avoiding coordination of their activities with potential allies such as candidates or political parties. The Federal Election Commission (FEC) issued a set of boundary lines that delineate what counts as an independent expenditure, and what counts as a coordinated one. A coordinated expenditure has taken place if a party or candidate suggests a particular communication to an independent expenditure-only committee; becomes "materially involved" in decision-making regarding the makeup of the advertisement; or participates in "substantial discussions" regarding the communication; uses the same vendor to produce the advertisement; or if a former employee of the candidate or party conveys relevant campaign information to the committee. Despite these rules, the boundary lines between an independent expenditure and a coordinated one can become rather blurry. For example, a super PAC can easily signal to an allied campaign its intentions to put up ads on a television station in a particular week, simply by placing an order that, by law, is publicly available. The campaign can access this information easily, and thus save its money for the following week. All this information can pass back and forth between super PAC and campaign without being counted as coordination (Farrar-Myers and Skinner 2012).

In 2012, super PACs debuted in the fight for the Republican nomination. On the one hand, they helped the rich get richer. Romney, whose own campaign raised the most money among all the Republican candidates, had a super PAC ally, Restore Our Future. At the end of 2011, when Gingrich surged in polls and appeared to be Romney's main threat, Restore Our Future launched attacks against him in order to stop his momentum. Ultimately, Restore Our Future spent almost $40 million in attacks against Romney's rivals for the nomination. On the other hand, super PACs played a large role in keeping Romney's main rivals for the nomination alive, deep into the primary season. Gingrich had his own super PAC ally, almost entirely underwritten by casino tycoon Sheldon Adelson and his family, which spent $17 million aiding his campaign. Santorum was assisted by the Red White and Blue Fund, which made $7.5 million in independent expenditures. Without the aid of these super PACs, it is difficult to imagine how Gingrich and Santorum could have raised the monies necessary to compete with Romney's superior fund-raising operation (for analysis of super PAC activity in the 2012 primaries, see Christenson and Smidt [2014]; Sebold et al. [2012] offer a picture of the political geography of Republican campaign financing). Thus far in 2015, super PACs appear ready to play a significantly larger role in the Republican nomination process. Jeb Bush, for example, delayed announcing his candidacy for months in order to be able to raise money for an allied super PAC without legal hindrance. Second-tier candidates such as businesswoman Carly Fiorina were offloading to super PAC allies many of the activities traditionally conducted by campaign organizations.

Money undoubtedly matters a great deal in presidential nomination contests, but it is important to keep in mind that early endorsements from the party's moneyed elites do not necessarily serve to crown one candidate as the winner. Giuliani and Romney in 2008 were the money kings, but neither was one of the final two candidates for the nomination because their messages were not acceptable to broad swaths of the GOP electorate. In short, moneyed elites matter only if they back a candidate whose message matters to voters.

More recent studies of the invisible primary have focused on the importance of political party elites to shaping nomination outcomes. During the invisible primary, rank-and-file voters take a back seat to the "nomination elite," which includes "officeholders, activists, resource providers, campaign specialists, media personnel, and the like" (Aldrich 2009). These elites form networks tightly organized (and polarized) by political party identification (Heaney et al. 2012; for early work on convention delegates, see Petrocik and Marvick [1983]). Presidential candidates seek to create campaign organizations that are representative of their political party at large—not just the "formal party organizations," but also the "informal networks" comprised of consultants, activists, donors, campaign professionals, and staff members of elected officials.

DOI: 10.1057/9781137577535.0006

Presidential campaigns are typically staffed by people possessing party connections and representing various factions of the party, rather than being wholly candidate-centered or representing just one faction. "The transition from factional, personalized candidates to party-oriented, coalition-seeking candidacies is the hallmark of the Expanded Party" (Bernstein and Dominguez 2003).

During the invisible primary, candidates consistently aim to portray themselves as better than their peers, whether by attacking an opponent, depicting the state of the horse race, or trumpeting endorsements (Haynes et al. 2002). In the absence of party identification as a cue, voters use candidate visibility and viability as their means of winnowing down the field of potential nominees. In order to appear viable, candidates must be able to contact many activists and voters during their campaigns. Party elites aid candidates in gaining the upper hand by helping them to build "extensive organizational and fundraising networks," as well as offering the media cues as to which campaigns are viable (Steger 2008; also see Feigenbaum and Shelton [2013]). These elites—who include not just elected officials, but "ideologues, fund-raisers, interest groups, and others"—engage in a "long-running national conversation" about which candidate "can best unite the party and win the next presidential election" (Cohen et al. 2008; also see Anderson [2013]). As the authors of one study, "The Viability Primary," put it:

> When party elites unify behind a candidate, they collectively send a signal to the news media, contributors, activists, and aligned groups about which candidate is viable, electable, and preferable. Heavily endorsed candidates are more likely to get on television, raise more funds, and solidify their support in national opinion polls prior to the primaries. When party elites coalesce early and strongly around the early favorite, that candidate has remained the front-runner during the pre-primary campaign and has gone on to win the nomination. (Dowdle et al. 2009)

Therefore, whether momentum matters during the primaries and caucuses depend on the outcome of the "invisible primary" that occurs before the contests begin (Steger 2008a). If a frontrunner fails to emerge, the percentage of undecided voters remains significant, and voter volatility remains high. Under such conditions, an early surprise performance in Iowa or New Hampshire can strongly influence the ultimate result. But when one candidate becomes the unquestioned leader of the pack and the nomination electorate already is approaching consensus, then early contests have a greater impact on who emerges as the chief

DOI: 10.1057/9781137577535.0006

challenger to the frontrunner, rather than the frontrunner himself. In the Republican primary cycles we cover in this volume, the best example of an invisible-primary elite consensus is that which supported George W. Bush's bid for the nomination in 2000.

All in all, scholars of the presidential nomination process reside in two camps on the importance of the "invisible primary," argues Wayne Steger (2013). Some propose that voters play no more than a "plebiscitary" role, confirming an agreement reached by "party elites, activists, donors, and groups" behind the scenes before the primaries and caucuses actually begin. The other camp places greater emphasis on candidates' performance during the caucuses and primaries, especially their ability to acquire momentum. Steger (2013) concludes that one or the other may dominate, depending on the particular characteristics of the nomination cycle. Sometimes elites and voters unify early, agreeing during the invisible primary on a frontrunner who then captures the nomination easily. This unity, however, is far from inevitable. In those cases, voters' decisions in early caucuses and primaries can be influential.

By no means do we dismiss the importance of party elites in winnowing the field of plausible nominees from which primary and caucus participants choose. We note, however, that an elite-based explanation of the outcome of recent Republican nomination contests leaves some questions unanswered. To say, for example, that "the party decided" in 2000 in favor of Bush is quite satisfactory. But the subsequent two Republican nomination contests are a more complicated story in which elites do not appear so dominant. During the run-up to the 2008 primaries and caucuses, McCain failed to garner significant financial advantages—and as Steger (2013) notes, McCain ultimately trailed Romney in elite endorsements. Nonetheless, McCain emerged as a most unlikely nominee, thanks in large part to the support of a party faction that lies outside the conservative mainstream. In 2012, more than three-quarters of Republican governors and Congressional members waited for Romney to become the clear frontrunner before making a commitment to him, despite the fact that his competitors for the nomination were less than formidable. The fact that in 2008 and 2012, more Republican party elites hesitated to endorse "is not consistent with the theoretical argument that political party insiders coordinate among themselves to pick their party's nominee" (Steger 2013). Party elite endorsements may be less important in recent elections because fewer elites are making them. This reticence may be attributed to lack of confidence in the candidates, or to division

DOI: 10.1057/9781137577535.0006

within the Republican coalition. In mid-October 2015, the majority of Republican elites were still watching from the sidelines.[3]

Bringing factions back in

Momentum-centered and elite-centered explanations of presidential nomination outcomes doubtless have their merits, yet fall short of being completely satisfactory. We propose to explain recent Republican nomination contests in terms of the voting behavior of factions that comprise today's GOP. The modern-day Republican Party is characterized by the persistence of internal factions (Reiter 2004). We will demonstrate that Republican Party voters may plausibly be divided into factions that, although they agree on much, have significant differences that define them. These differences drove the dynamics of the Republican nomination contest in recent history, and we are confident they will do so again in 2016. In the following chapters, we propose that the Republican Party contains four discrete factions that are based primarily on ideology, with elements of class and religious background tempering that focus. These factions are: moderate and liberal voters; "somewhat conservative" voters; very conservative evangelical voters; and very conservative secular voters.

The foundations for our analysis are rooted in the earliest studies of the presidential nomination process in the 1970s. Steven Brams (1978) argued that candidates' positions on public policy issues are an important factor for presidential primary voters. Brams assumed that candidates' positions on a given issue, as well as the attitudes of party voters, could be placed on a left-right, liberal-conservative continuum. Most candidates are labeled as liberal, moderate, or conservative, and voters choose a candidate whose position most closely matches their own. As a result, candidates choose issue positions that attract the most voters.

A multicandidate primary is noteworthy for its instability. In a two-person primary, both candidates find the middle, or "median," issue position to be best, regardless of the opponent's position because it ensures the candidate will win 50 percent of the vote. In a primary with multiple candidates, however, adopting the median position is no guarantee of success. Rival candidates may adopt positions to the right or left of the centrist candidates and attract a plurality. Policy positions that are secure in a two-candidate race are invariably vulnerable in a

DOI: 10.1057/9781137577535.0006

multicandidate contest. A new candidate may always find a position that disrupts a proximate candidate's chances of success. For instance, a moderate candidate's best position is not the midway point between two opponents on his left and right, but rather a position "closer to his less extreme opponent" (Brams 1978). A "centrist" candidate in a primary faces potential opponents among more liberal candidates and more conservative candidates, both of whom may encroach on the electorate's center. If a candidate finds the middle crowded with competitors, then he may be better served to line up to the right of the so-called median voter. This move enables the right-of-center candidate to pick up more moderate voters, as more centrist candidates drop out. In the attrition game of the presidential nomination process, a candidate has to consider other candidates' strategies: "Winning depends on the choices that *all* players make" (Brams 1978). The multicandidate primary becomes especially complicated if there are multiple significant issues in a campaign (also see Aldrich [1980] and Norrander [1986]; for later work on spatial voting models in nomination contests, see Kenny and Lotfinia [2005]).

If a candidate makes a clear statement on an issue, it will attract some voters, while alienating others who find themselves a significant distance from that candidate's issue-position. To avoid alienating voters, candidates sometimes make ambiguous statements in order to set up "fuzzy" positions that cover a range of possibilities on the ideological spectrum, not just a single point. Adopting a "fuzzy" position is not without risk. Voters might judge that the candidate's actual position is farther from them, not nearer. They also might judge the candidate's ambiguity to be cowardly, rather than flexible (Brams 1978). A "fuzzy" position may work best for a candidate who is trying to reach out toward voters on the extremes, while keeping more moderate voters loyal with more centrist positions. But that candidate with fuzzy centrist positions might face encroachments from both his left and his right on his support among centrist voters, especially if they can be persuaded that his fuzzy statements mask extreme positions (Brams 1978).

One additional benefit to candidates for taking ambiguous positions stems from the sequential nature of the presidential nomination process. Primary candidates must perform well over a series of contests, not just one election. Primaries do not select candidates so much as they eliminate or "winnow" them. Candidates, of course, seek to avoid elimination. When there are multiple candidates in the primary, candidates must avoid defeat by others who seek to gain support from the same part of

DOI: 10.1057/9781137577535.0006

the party electorate (Brams 1978; for a case study of how primary voters made strategic choices in the 1988 primaries, see Cain et al. [1989]). In later primaries, survivors tend to be spaced farther apart ideologically than in the early rounds. Candidates thus have reason to make their issue positions more ambiguous in order to attract voters who might otherwise be alienated because their positions are at some distance from the positions of the remaining candidates. They do, however, run the risk of being labeled "wishy-washy or evasive." As a result, candidates will both "hew to basic positions" but also "scamper for pockets of support somewhat removed from these positions" (Brams 1978).

Brams provides the foundation for our analysis as follows: Primary and caucus voters seek candidates whose issue positions are closest to their own. Candidates take issue positions with an eye toward attracting voters. Multicandidate primaries are inherently unstable. Candidates may focus early on securing the support of a particular party faction, but wish to retain the flexibility to build a coalition in later stages of the nomination contest. In later contests in the sequential nomination process, voters may have fewer candidates from which to choose. This makes their decision easier, but also means they may have to settle for a candidate who is not their favorite.

Does ideology matter to presidential primary voters?

Readers may reasonably object that Brams overestimated primary voters' ability to make ideological distinctions between candidates of the same party, especially in a crowded field. Political scientists warn that rank-and-file voters should not be confused with ideologically minded activists. Elites in the Republican nomination process have been long recognized for their attention to ideology. Battles between the Right and the non-Right date back to the mid-20th century (Costain 1980). In particular, "amateur" activists have been regarded as "more ideologically extreme" and "willing to put principle above party," compared to the more pragmatic professional class, dedicated to the party's success in winning political office. Amateurs tend to hold more conservative beliefs than the professional political class. These activists also may disagree about whether pivoting toward the moderate, median voter or embracing conservative "conviction politicians" such as Ronald Reagan is the best route toward electoral success (Clarke

DOI: 10.1057/9781137577535.0006

et al. 1991; also see McCann [1995]). Political activists, such as convention delegates, also tend to display ideological consistency. They use
terms such as "liberal" and "conservative" correctly in political debates
and in the structure of their own beliefs (Herrera 1992). Political elites'
ability to think ideologically does not necessarily imply that a candidate's ideology is their foremost concern. A survey of 1980 convention
delegates found that Republican activists prioritized a candidate's electability over his ideology in picking a nominee. Reagan, for example,
had the backing of half of self-described liberals and moderates, despite
the fact that George H. W. Bush was a better ideological fit for those
delegates. Reagan was overwhelmingly seen as more electable than
Bush. Ideological fit mattered only in cases when delegates discerned
no difference between Reagan and Bush's electability. Perhaps surprisingly, it was Bush who was the "ideological" candidate, inasmuch as
a plurality of Bush delegates supported him because of his ideology,
despite regarding Reagan as "more electable." The authors noted that
more extreme ideology and electability were not necessarily incom-
patible: "Moderation in the pursuit of victory is not always a virtue.
Giving the voters a choice and not an echo is sometimes pragmatic
strategy" (Stone and Abramowitz 1983).

Compared to activists, primary voters' ability to use ideology to make
choices among candidates of the same party is uncertain. Early critics
of the primary-centered nomination process argued that primary voters
were "highly ideological," but political scientists have found a variety of
evidence that presidential primary voters are not especially so. Using
national survey data, Norrander (1989) demonstrated that significant
differences between primary voters and general election voters were
rare. On the one hand, Republican voters were more likely to "discuss
politics in terms of ideology" than general-election Republican voters.
But evidence that primary voters were more consistent in their beliefs
was lacking. So was evidence that primary voters develop ideological
identifications (akin to party identifications) that act as lenses through
which they see the political world and lead them to choose candidates
with similar "ideological labels." In fact, in contrast to activists, the
general public's set of "political preferences and perspectives" is far less
"constrained and stable"—even among those most closely engaged in
politics. Voters' ideological responses tend to be riddled with "misun-
derstandings, top of the head responses, order effects, poor retention,
and various satisficing strategies" (Jennings 1992). Lau (2013) finds that

DOI: 10.1057/9781137577535.0006

primary voters are not good at finding "the candidate who represents their own values and concerns."

Other scholars argue that voters use ideology more robustly in making presidential nomination decisions. Ideology may not only help to shape voter preferences, but also their views on issues, as well as what they think of candidates' qualities (Kenney and Rice 1992). For instance, "An ideological vote, like a party vote, may reflect group support and loyalty." When voters perceive they are ideologically closer to a particular candidate, they vote accordingly. For example, the relationship between a voter's ideology and their choice of Reagan in 1980 strengthened in cases in which a voter perceived Reagan as ideologically to the right of his opponents (Wattier 1983). Although voters may be uncertain about the specific issue positions of various candidates, they still can use ideology as a "general-choice rule," comparing the ideologies of candidates and choosing the candidate whose ideology best matches their own. But voters can only take this "short cut" if candidates present differing ideologies in a way perceivable to voters. It is also possible that voters might "project" their own ideology onto the candidate of their choice. Or a candidate might convince voters to accept his ideology as their own (Downs 1957; Wattier 1983; Kenney 1993; Popkin 1994).

Still others state that other factors outweigh the importance of ideology to primary voters' choice of candidates (Mayer 2008, for instance). Voters' perceptions of the personal qualities of candidates, for instance, have been shown to play a more significant role in their choices. In addition, voters may find it difficult to choose candidates according to their positions on issues because they do not readily recognize candidates and gathering information on policy positions is costly in terms of voter time and attention. Candidates deliberately minimize their differences in order to keep the door open to supporters of opponents who drop out. In addition, media spend more time writing "horse race" stories about where candidates stand in the polls, rather than discussing policy differences among the candidates (Marshall 1984; Aldrich 1980).

Setting aside the shortfalls of voters and media, presidential candidates of the same party ideologically resemble each other much more closely now than they did in previous decades. Paulson (2009) argues, for instance, that the political polarization of the two major parties has also created "ideological homogenization" within fields of presidential primary candidates. Conservatism is obviously the dominant ideology of the Republican Party, just as liberalism dominates the Democratic

DOI: 10.1057/9781137577535.0006

Party. Half a century ago, liberal and moderate Republicans such as Nelson Rockefeller were power brokers who resisted the conservative movement led by Barry Goldwater until the party's convention. But by 1980, moderates readily accepted Ronald Reagan as their nominee after their candidate, George H. W. Bush, failed in his primary campaign. In 2000 and 2008, for instance, McCain was the favorite of moderate and liberal voters, but he nonetheless took conservative positions on a variety of issues. If parties were still as ideologically diverse as they were in the twentieth century, conventions would still be the site of furious floor fights over nominations, despite the changes in delegate-selection rules.

Nonetheless, scholars have found evidence that candidates take ideology into account during their primary campaigns. A study of candidate advertising strategies in the 2004 and 2008 presidential nomination campaigns found that conservative candidates in Republican primaries were more likely to run negative advertising against liberal and moderate primary opponents instead of fellow conservatives who shared a common voter base. The authors hypothesized that candidates might be avoiding such criticism in order to forestall ill feelings that might affect their ability to get out their base in the general election. More simply, conservative candidates might find more to criticize in the positions of their moderate and liberal counterparts, rather than their fellow conservatives (Ridout and Holland 2010; for more on candidate strategy, see Ridout et al. [2009]. Haynes and Rhine [1998], however, found that candidates' attack strategies had much more to do with their standing in the race, than ideology; also see Meirick et al. [2011]).

In terms of ultimate outcomes, recent scholarship has shown that the more ideological a candidate, the larger the candidate's share of the primary vote after New Hampshire, even after accounting for other factors such as national polls taken prior to the Iowa caucus, elite endorsements, and the results in early contests (Steger 2008a). There is some initial evidence that social media interactions mostly take place among individuals who possess similar political views, suggesting that ideology is a means to bind voters together (Barbera 2015).

How ideology guides voters

In the following chapters, we argue that Republican primary voters' ideology is an important ingredient that distinguishes one faction of voters

DOI: 10.1057/9781137577535.0006

from others. Ideology, we argue, extends much further in organizing voters' thoughts than preferences for a particular set of issue positions. Using evidence from exit poll data, we will argue that Republican voters of different ideologies (from liberal and moderate, to somewhat conservative, to very conservative) wish for different *personal characteristics* in their candidates. In addition, although Republican voters may have similar sets of positions on issues, they disagree amongst themselves as to *which issues should receive the highest priority* from their prospective nominee. We also find that ideology intermingles with voters' *value priorities*. Although religious voters tend to favor the Republican candidate in general elections, we find that Republican primary voters are significantly at odds amongst themselves about the proper role of religion in guiding public policy. Finally, candidate *viability* is a priority for voters, especially in the middle and later rounds of the nomination process.

Personal characteristics of the candidate

While the topic has not been widely explored by scholars, there is some evidence that voters with different ideologies may seek candidates with differing personal qualities. For example, a study of primary voters in 1988 and 2000 found that Republican and conservative primary voters appear to be attracted to candidates who have a reputation for moral virtue, while liberals and Democrats are more interested in candidates who exhibit compassion (Barker et al. 2006). One has to consider the possibility, however, that rather than a voter's assessment of the candidate driving his vote, that a voter who has already chosen a candidate will change his assessment of his qualities in a correspondingly more positive direction (Campbell 1983).

Primary voters and candidate priorities

Aldrich and Alvarez (1994) argue that although candidates for the nomination tend to differ little when it comes to policy positions, candidates' policy *priorities* are important markers to voters. In other words, primary voters are interested in knowing "Which candidate has priorities that most closely match my own?" Often candidates address policies by asserting which problems they view as most important, which they will

DOI: 10.1057/9781137577535.0006

focus on if elected. For example, in 1988, budget deficits became known as Bob Dole's issue, not because other Republicans were not also against them, but because his reputation, as well as his campaign's messaging, made him appear most likely to make deficit reduction a top priority if elected. A candidate uses policy statements to convince voters that their concerns are his concerns, and that the candidate will be committed to solve problems important to them if elected.

Campaigns allocate their resources in order to highlight particular characteristics of the candidate. Issue-based campaigns seek issues on which voters in the target electorate have a high degree of consensus, and on which they can convince voters that opponents hold the minority position. Candidates that make issue appeals risk becoming divisive, and may find "consensual themes" a less risky way to appeal to voters. Candidates from the same party often differ little in their issue positions, and are appealing to primary electorates that are also rather homogenous. The 1976 Republican presidential primary between Gerald Ford and Ronald Reagan, as fierce as it was rhetorically, did not prove that so-called issue-voting had great effect (Page 1976, 1978; Gopoian 1982).

The presence of many candidates in a primary, plus lack of "intraparty differentiation," leads to relatively low voter knowledge of where candidates stand on issues, and "little choice" based on issue-positions. Since candidates largely agree on policy positions, the key question is what issues candidates will grant the "highest priority." If voters believe presidents are elected to solve important issues, then candidates' priorities are employed by voters to evaluate them. Voters' concern with policy priorities indicates a primary electorate more sophisticated than mere "political predispositions toward a candidate"; voters are capable of identifying candidates who have similar concerns to theirs (Aldrich and Alvarez 1994; also see Petrocik 1996; Hillygus and Henderson 2010).

Candidate values as guides for voters

Marietta and Barker (2007) argue that values, defined as "core normative predispositions," or "abstract visions of the 'good,'" have a significant effect on primary voters' decisions. These values guide them even in cases when they have little knowledge or sophistication. Primary voters face the dilemma of choosing a candidate without the cue of party identification as a guide. An internal compass for voters is their "value priorities," which makes discerning between candidates easier, and allows "even relatively unsophisticated voters to cast meaningfully representative votes." These values are best described as "core normative predispositions," or "abstract visions of the 'good'" that enable voters to set priorities, even between opposing goods such as liberty and morality. Armed with knowledge of their own value priorities, voters can then discern which of the primary candidates hold similar priorities. This discernment would aid voters in making their decisions (Marietta and Barker 2007). For instance, Republican primary voters respond more positively to candidates who are viewed as individualists, as opposed to egalitarians (Barker 2005).

One such competition of opposing values is over where citizens look for truth. Do they rely on "religious faith," or "scientific evidence and reason" (Marietta and Barker 2007)? This dispute, which lies at the heart of the "culture war," also is a fault line within the modern Republican Party electorate, which contains both philosophical libertarians and Christian fundamentalists. For example, voters who thought that scientific knowledge was more important for the social good than religious faith were more likely to vote for McCain in 2000 than George W. Bush.

Candidate viability

Some primary voters vote sincerely, that is, they vote for the candidate they like best, without weighing the candidate's chances of winning. Others vote in a strategic or sophisticated manner, weighing both their personal preferences and the candidates' odds of winning. Such voters would consider a less-preferred candidate who is more viable and has a greater chance of winning the nomination of their party (Abramson et al. 1992; but also see Grafstein [2003]).

Collingwood et al. (2012) argue that a candidate's perceived chances of winning the nomination, or "viability," have tended to be underestimated as a factor in models of presidential primary voting (for earlier studies of viability, see Abramowitz [1987 and 1989]; Guerrant and Gurian [1996]). Candidate performance in the first contests of the nomination season are likely to change perceptions and evaluations of that candidate in later contests, which in turn affect the candidate's level of support. For instance, Barack Obama's strong early performance in 2008 led undecided voters and even those who supported other candidates to view him as more viable. As a result, many shifted their support to him. Momentum remains significant, especially when the party does not reach consensus on a favorite before voters begin to have their say in Iowa and New Hampshire. But it also matters whether various party factions have more or less of a presence in various states in the sequence of primaries and caucuses. The sequence of primaries helps to determine "which party factions will have an ideologically compatible candidate in the race" after the first contests for the nomination. Occasionally primary voters employ "retrospective voting" in their decision-making, especially in the first part of the nomination process (for earlier research on retrospective voting, see Monardi [1994]). Factors such as the perceived state of the economy, and one's own "personal finances," are important. These variables, however, lose effect in the later stages of the contest.

Summing up: faction and friction

In this book, we argue that party factions are not just a matter of ideology, but more broadly, a matter of political identity for primary voters. Party factions will seek a candidate who holds their values and priorities as his or her values and priorities. In short, they seek a champion. Voters look not just for candidates with similar values and priorities, but also for success. An early victory cements the relationship, that is, a faction bonds with a candidate who earns the title of its champion by virtue of his or her performance in early nomination contests. Voters desire a candidate who exhibits electoral strength, but they also want a strong candidate who is "one of their own." A candidate will reap the benefits of momentum most acutely (and most quickly) among voters who perceive that the candidate shares their values and priorities, their issue positions, and even a common cultural and political identity.

While momentum has long been recognized as a phenomenon in the nomination process, *friction* explains the phenomenon by which certain factions adhere to a particular candidate over time. And once they adhere, they are reluctant to let go, even after the candidate's prospects begin to fade. The more the group feels like outsiders in the party, the stronger the friction – for instance, scholars have found evidence of "boomerang" or "underdog" effects which counter momentum. "When exposed to the contradictory opinions of others, a person strongly committed to his or her viewpoint would be most likely to generate counter-arguments

DOI: 10.1057/9781137577535.0006

defending his or her initial position." Thus the presence of opposition only increases the person's adherence to her original views (Mutz 1997; Geer 1988; Kaplowitz 1983; Patterson 1980).

As a result of friction, momentum for presidential primary candidates does not work across the board, attracting all party factions equally. This means that some surges of candidate momentum may be less potent and long-lasting than others. For it is one thing for a candidate to become the champion of a faction, and another to be able to build bridges to voters of other factions, in order to create a coalition that can capture the nomination. In fact, voters from other factions may react adversely to the success of a candidate from a rival faction, and seek to create friction in order to slow that candidate's momentum. The desire to stop a candidate may lead voters from other factions to join forces and accept a second-best alternative—a candidate who is viable, and closer to that group's ideal mix of issue-positions and priorities.

In the following chapters, we will argue that in the absence of a consensus frontrunner, Republican voters seek a viable candidate who best represents their issue positions and priorities. In the early contests, candidates compete not only to be the frontrunner of the field, but also to become the champion of their particular faction. Only factional champions possess the voter base that enables them to compete in later rounds of the nomination process. In this respect, the nomination contest resembles the rounds of the national collegiate basketball tournament, in which candidates appealing to similar voter groups must first survive their bracket in order to advance to the final rounds (Cook 2011). It is this sequential game that we will explore in the chapters ahead.

Methodology and exit polls

The chapters to follow are largely based on voter data compiled from exit polls taken after Republican primaries and caucuses in 2000, 2008, and 2012, now stored at the Roper Center for Public Opinion Research. (We also occasionally use national polls of Republican primary voters, fielded by Gallup or the Pew Research Center, in order to offer a snapshot of the national primary electorate at a particular point in time.) All exit poll data are weighted according to the pollsters' prescriptions.

Studies of presidential primary voters do not often make use of exit polls (but see Mayer [2008]; McKee and Hayes [2009]) but there are

DOI: 10.1057/9781137577535.0006

compelling reasons to do so. First, exit polls survey actual voters as they leave their polling places. As a result, they avoid the typical polling dilemma of determining who is likely to vote and who is unlikely to do so. Second, respondents to exit polls record their own answers on questionnaires confidentially, without having to report them directly to the interviewer, as is the case with telephone surveys. Last but not least, exit polls collect data from a far larger number of respondents than telephone surveys. Whereas a national telephone survey might reach several hundred respondents, exit pollsters often contacted more than 1,000 from a single primary or caucus state. As a result, when we weighted and pooled the data from various primaries and caucuses held in a given cycle, we were able to examine subgroups within the Republican primary electorate, such as "somewhat conservative" voters or very conservative evangelicals (Best and Krueger 2012).

Exit polls do have problems. Like all surveys, they take samples of the electorate, and thus are subject to sampling error. In addition, exit polls use stratified sampling, which adds an additional element of variability. (However, the larger sample sizes of exit polls lower sampling error.) Exit polls are also subject to coverage error because interviewers sometimes make mistakes in applying the rates by which they interview potential respondents. Perhaps most worrisome is nonresponse error, when a respondent selected for the sample does not complete the survey. If it were the case that groups of Republicans complete surveys at different rates, then overall results could be biased (Best and Krueger 2012). Exit poll questionnaires also tend to be limited in their range of questions beyond voter choice and the standard set of demographic queries. Questions may vary not only from election cycle to election cycle, but from contest to contest within a particular cycle.

In 2000, Republican primary electorates in 26 states were polled. They included: Arizona, California, Colorado, Connecticut, Delaware, Florida, Georgia, Iowa, Louisiana, Massachusetts, Maine, Maryland, Michigan, Mississippi, Missouri, New Hampshire, New York, Ohio, Oklahoma, Rhode Island, South Carolina, Tennessee, Texas, Utah, Vermont, and Virginia.

In 2008, Republican primary electorates in 29 states were surveyed. They included: Alabama, Arkansas, Arizona, California, Connecticut, Delaware, Florida, Georgia, Iowa, Illinois, Louisiana, Massachusetts, Maryland, Michigan, Mississippi, Missouri, New Hampshire, New York,

DOI: 10.1057/9781137577535.0006

New Jersey, Nevada, Ohio, Oklahoma, South Carolina, Tennessee, Texas, Utah, Vermont, Virginia, and Wisconsin.

In 2012, Republican primary electorates in 20 states were polled. They included: Alabama, Arizona, Florida, Georgia, Iowa, Illinois, Louisiana, Massachusetts, Maryland, Michigan, Mississippi, New Hampshire, Nevada, Ohio, Oklahoma, South Carolina, Tennessee, Vermont, Virginia, and Wisconsin.

All told, the exit polls surveyed 33 states over the three cycles of 2000, 2008, and 2012. We have data on the Republican electorates in 28 of the first 45 contests on the provisional 2016 Republican nomination calendar, according to the website Frontloading HQ.

Notes

1   We are by no means the first to offer a picture of the Republican Party as a coalition of factions. In the 1990s, for example, Nicol Rae offered a far-seeing portrait of the then-emerging Republican factions in the years after Ronald Reagan (Shafer 1998). These factions included "traditional Republicans," who hailed from the Midwest and had the backing of small businesses and the Chamber of Commerce; but also "populist conservatives" (culturally conservative, intensely nationalistic blue-collar workers), the "religious right," and "supply-side libertarians" led by tax-cut enthusiasts such as Jack Kemp and Steve Forbes. Our analysis differs from Rae's in important respects, such as the continued importance of moderate and even liberal Republicans in presidential nomination contests; our analytical categories, in addition, allow for Republican primary voting behavior to be studied more easily. Our study also confirms the enduring strength of the party factions that Rae correctly perceived to be emerging two decades ago.

2   "Romney campaign spent $18.50 per vote." http://money.cnn. com/2012/04/25/news/economy/Romney-campaign-spending-vote/ Accessed October 20, 2015.

3   See FiveThirtyEight.com's scoreboard of endorsements, http://projects. fivethirtyeight.com/2016-endorsement-primary/. Accessed October 20, 2015.

DOI: 10.1057/9781137577535.0006

2

Moderate and Liberal Republican Primary Voters

Abstract: *The moderate or liberal bloc of the Republican Party is surprisingly strong in presidential years, comprising the second-largest voting bloc with approximately 25–30 percent of all GOP voters nationwide. They are especially strong in early voting states such as New Hampshire (where they have comprised between 45 and 49 percent of the GOP electorate between 1996 and 2012), Florida, and Michigan. Moderates and liberals tend to prefer presidential candidates who are independent-minded and keep politics separate from religion. Although the GOP is known as a conservative party, the choice of moderates and liberals has ultimately emerged as the nominee in the last two nomination cycles.*

Keywords: ideology, presidential elections, presidential primaries, Republican Party

Olsen, Henry, and Dante J. Scala. *The Four Faces of the Republican Party: The Fight for the 2016 Presidential Nomination.* New York: Palgrave Macmillan, 2016. DOI: 10.1057/9781137577535.0007.

In this chapter, we address the role moderate and liberal voters have played in Republican presidential primaries since 2000. Specifically, we establish that this bloc of voters is significantly more secular than more conservative voters. They hold a distinctive position on abortion, an issue of great importance to the party. Further, although moderates and liberals do agree with more conservative Republicans on a number of issues, their issue priorities are unique among primary voters. We then demonstrate that these voters do behave as a cohesive bloc during the nomination season.

While moderates and liberals are a minority within the Republican Party, they make the most of their numbers by rallying behind a single candidate very early in the nomination process. The first-in-the-nation New Hampshire primary is a crucial catalyst to their success. Its electorate is tailor-made for the success of a moderate Republican: Candidates who succeed in attracting the lion's share of moderates there have an excellent chance of winning the primary outright. The winner of the New Hampshire primary is also guaranteed the rapid communication of his personal qualities and ideas nationally. As a result, a candidate who succeeds in persuading New Hampshire's moderate Republicans becomes overnight the leader of the moderate/liberal faction nationally. The early bonding of Republican moderates and liberals to a single champion of their values gives their candidate a fighting chance against more conservative opponents, even though he leads a minority faction.

The presence of moderate and liberal voters in Republican primaries

The moderate or liberal bloc is surprisingly strong in presidential years, comprising the second-largest voting bloc with approximately 25–30 percent of all Republican voters nationwide. Their turnout (and influence) in Republican primaries has decreased over the past decade, but they remain an important bloc for candidates to consider. In recent cycles, they have been especially strong in early voting states such as New Hampshire (where they have comprised between 45 and 49 percent of the GOP electorate between 1996 and 2012), Florida, and Michigan. They are, however, surprisingly numerous even in the Deep South, the most conservative portion of the country.

DOI: 10.1057/9781137577535.0007

It was not so long ago that moderates and liberals comprised a near-majority of Republican primary voters in a significant number of primaries. Of the 26 states in which exit polls were conducted in 2000, moderates and liberals comprised 40 percent or more of the Republican electorate in half of them. Only 2 states had less than 30 percent.

A comparison of exit polls in 2000 and 2012 shows that this bloc of voters diminished over the past decade, but still remained significant in numerous states. In 2012, moderates and liberals exceeded 40 percent of the primary electorate in just four states of the 20 exit-polled, but this bloc remained larger than 30 percent in ten other states.

One of the two states with the smallest presence of moderates and liberals is the first-in-the-nation caucus state of Iowa. Although Iowa Republicans have a simple straw poll (as opposed to the complex and lengthy meetings that Iowa Democrats endure on caucus night), participation rates tend to be low. Some 122,000 Republicans participated in the 2012 caucuses; more than 600,000 voters in Iowa are registered Republicans. Not coincidentally, the caucus tends to attract the most enthusiastic, ideologically conservative Iowans. In the 2000 caucus, the bloc of moderate and liberal voters in Iowa comprised just one of four voters; only Louisiana had so few. Twelve years later, that bloc had shrunk to just one of six voters in Iowa, a decrease of more than one-third of its voting power.

In contrast, the second event on the calendar, New Hampshire's first in the nation primary, possesses one of the largest blocs of moderate and liberal voters: 48 percent of all Republican primary voters in 2012, essentially unchanged since 2000. Its contest is open to voters registered "undeclared," who refuse to disclose their party affiliation or do not possess one. New Hampshire's undeclared voters may ask for either a Republican or Democratic primary ballot, and then revert back to "undeclared" on their way out of the polling place. In 2012, almost a quarter million voters went to the polls there to cast votes in the Republican primary.

The South (Figure 2.1) is rightly regarded as the most conservative part of the Republican Party. But almost one-third of voters casting ballots in South Carolina, the first southern state to vote in the presidential nomination contest, describe themselves as moderates or liberals. Moderates or liberals have comprised between 31 and 39 percent of the South Carolina electorate since 1996, outnumbering or roughly equaling very conservative voters in each of those years. They wield similar voting power in Florida. Compared to other regions, liberals and moderates

DOI: 10.1057/9781137577535.0007

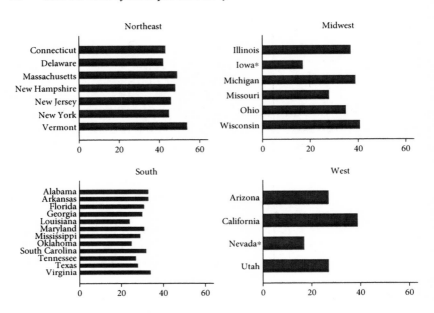

FIGURE 2.1   *Presence of moderates and liberals in Republican primaries and caucuses*

*Caucus state

Source: Weighted exit poll data, 2008 and 2012.

hold the least voting power in Southern presidential primaries, but still typically cast three of 10 ballots.

Aside from the Iowa caucus electorate, moderate and liberal voters wield a considerable amount of influence in the Midwest. This bloc of voters typically comprises 35–40 percent of the electorate, according to exit polls taken in 2008 and 2012.

Moderate and liberal voters are most numerous in the Northeast, where they typically comprise almost half the Republican primary electorate. New England states such as Massachusetts and Vermont top the list in this region.

In the West, the presence of moderate and liberal voters varies dramatically in the few states in which recent exit polls have been taken. They were least influential in the Nevada caucuses, in which they constituted just one of six voters. They were most numerous in California, where they comprised four of ten voters.

To sum up, while casual observers are correct in their assumption that moderates and liberals are outnumbered by conservatives in the national

DOI: 10.1057/9781137577535.0007

Republican presidential primary electorate, they may be surprised by how large a minority these voters constitute. As one might expect, Republican moderates and liberals are most prominent on the East and West coasts, but they are an important presence in the Midwest as well. Even in the South, the most conservative region of the Republican Party, moderates and liberals are not an insignificant force if they unite behind a single candidate. The following sections consider how much Republican moderates and liberals hold in common, in terms of their values, priorities, and the qualities they desire to see in a candidate.

Moderate and liberal Republican primary voters: preferences and priorities

Exit polls from 2000 to 2012 reveal a bloc of voters with a distinctive set of candidate preferences and issue priorities. They are, first and foremost, most likely to describe themselves as independent-minded, and seek candidates who profess to be the same. While they are not gadflies, they tend to be attracted to candidates who are self-proclaimed tellers of difficult truths that challenge party orthodoxy. They are much more secular than more conservative primary voters, and steer clear of candidates who are the champions of religious conservatives. Moderate and liberal voters prefer someone who is both more secular and less fiscally conservative than their somewhat conservative cousins.

In 1996, for example, they preferred Tennessee Senator Lamar Alexander over Bob Dole.[1] In 2000, they were the original McCainiacs, supporting a candidate who backed campaign-finance regulation, opposed tax cuts for the top bracket, and criticized the influence of evangelical leader Pat Robertson. In 2008, they stuck with John McCain, giving him their crucial backing in New Hampshire and providing his margin of victory in virtually every state. In 2012, many moderate and liberal voters began firmly in Texas Congressman Ron Paul's or former Utah Governor Jon Huntsman's camp. Paul and Huntsman combined got 43 percent of their vote in Iowa and 50 percent in New Hampshire. Once it became clear that their candidates could not win, however, moderates or liberals who were not diehard Paulites swung firmly toward Romney in his fights with Newt Gingrich and Rick Santorum.

DOI: 10.1057/9781137577535.0007

TABLE 2.1   *Profile of moderate and liberal Republican voters*

		Moderates and liberals	Other GOP primary voters
PARTY IDENTIFICATION			
Identify as Republican?	2008	61	83
	2012	49	77
TEA PARTY			
Support Tea Party	2012	32	73
ABORTION			
Should abortion be legal in most or all cases?	2008	55	23
	2012	58	24
ISSUES			
Which issue mattered most in 2008?	Economy	49	35
	War in Iraq	22	17
	Illegal immigration	16	25
Which issues mattered most in 2012?	Economy	64	51
	Budget deficit	22	30
	Abortion	5	11
CANDIDATE QUALITIES			
Which mattered most?	Shares my values	34	50
2008	Says what he believes	29	21
	Right experience	27	20
2012	Able to defeat Obama	33	42
	Right experience	27	17
	Strong moral character	24	19
	True conservative	8	19

Source: Pooled and weighted exit poll data from primaries and caucuses, 2008 and 2012. N. B.: Total number of respondents in 2008: 25,973; in 2012: 38,010. The number of respondents for each question, however, did vary.

Party identification

The simplest sign of the ambivalence of moderates and liberals toward the Republican Party is their self-described party identification (Table 2.1). Liberal and moderate voters were the least likely to identify themselves as Republicans, compared to more conservative primary voters. In 2012, for instance, just about half described themselves as Republicans,

DOI: 10.1057/9781137577535.0007

compared to strong majorities of more conservative voters. Although self-identified Republicans always outnumbered independents among this bloc of voters, liberals and moderates were most likely to identify themselves as independents.

Although moderates and liberals have mixed feelings toward the Republican Party, they should not be confused with Tea Partiers, who arose in the early days of the Obama Administration partly in response to the massive government intervention intended to reverse the Great Recession of fall 2008. By 2012, the Tea Party had become shorthand for a fiercely populist, antiestablishment brand of conservatism. In 2012, liberals and moderates were the least likely to be supportive of this movement. Only a minority expressed support, compared to strong majorities of more conservative primary voters.

Liberals and moderates: candidate qualities

One perennial question in primary exit polls is what candidate quality mattered most to voters. Unsurprisingly, compared to their more conservative peers, liberals and moderates were least likely in 2012 to say it was most important that the candidate was a "true conservative." More so than more conservative voters, liberals and moderates were more likely to stress the candidate's strength of moral character, and whether the candidate had the "right experience."

In 2008, liberals and moderates were more likely than more conservative voters to say that the most important quality about a candidate was that the candidate "says what he believes." They were least likely to state that it was most important that a candidate "shares my values."

In 2000, liberals and moderates were more likely than their more conservative peers to say that a candidate who stands up for his beliefs was the quality that mattered most in their voting decisions. They also were more likely to give high marks to a candidate who was a "strong leader." They were much less likely than more conservative voters to say that representing "conservative values" was the quality that mattered most. In all, these voters were most likely to say that the person, not the ideology, mattered most.

DOI: 10.1057/9781137577535.0007

The secularism of liberals and moderates

Although the Republican Party is widely known as the "religious party" (compared to the Democrats' secularism), the moderate or liberal Republican voter tends to be attracted to candidates who wish to keep politics separate from religion. Time and again, majorities of this bloc of voters support the Republican candidate who seems least overtly religious and are motivated to oppose the candidate who is most overtly religious. This makes them a secure bank of votes for a somewhat conservative candidate who emerges from the early stages of the primary season in a battle with a religious conservative, as occurred in 1996, 2008, and 2012.

This tendency makes sense when one considers these voters' description of their own religious behavior. In 2008 and 2012, only a third described themselves as born-again or evangelical Christians. In 2008, this group was much less likely to attend religious services once a week (or more), compared to more conservative Republican primary voters. Many moderate and liberal Republicans do not view religion as central to their lives, and do not wish for religion to be central to their party's politics.

Their relative lack of religiosity leads these voters to downplay the importance of religion in politics. For example, in 2000 only a small minority of moderate and liberal voters identified themselves with the religiously conservative movement known as the "religious right." In 2012, they were significantly less likely to say that it mattered a great deal that a candidate shared their religious beliefs, compared to more conservative Republican primary voters.

The secularism of moderate and liberal Republican primary voters translates into significant contrasts on issue positions with their fellow partisans. Although Republican primary voters typically agree on issue positions far more often than they disagree, moderate and liberal Republican primary voters clearly disagree with their conservative copartisans on the issue of abortion. In 2000, 2008, and 2012, a majority of moderates and liberals stated that abortion should be legal, compared to the minorities of more conservative Republicans. Only a small minority of moderates and liberals said that abortion should be outlawed entirely. Moderates and liberals also were least likely to name abortion as their top priority in deciding how to vote in the presidential primaries. Just 1 out of 10 did so in 2000, and 1 out of 20 said the same in 2012.

DOI: 10.1057/9781137577535.0007

Moderates and liberals: issue priorities

In 2000, moderates and liberals were more likely than more conservative primary voters to mention Social Security, education, and campaign
finance reform as their most important issues. They were less likely to
mention moral values – a choice apparently inserted in response to
public concerns regarding Bill Clinton's White House sex scandal.

In 2008, moderates and liberals were most likely to cite the economy
as the most pressing concern facing the country. A distant second was
the war in Iraq. They were least likely to mention terrorism as the most
important issue.

In 2012, most moderates and liberals again said the economy was the
issue that mattered most in their voting decisions. A distant second was
the federal budget deficit.

Illegal immigration was another issue that caused moderates and
liberals very little concern. In 2008, immigration was mentioned as the
top priority far less often than other options. Four years later, the issue
had receded even further for them. In both years, however, moderates
and liberals were the GOP faction likeliest to support giving illegal
immigrants a path to citizenship or permanent legal residence.

To sum up: liberals and moderates have found themselves on the
margins of a party that has only grown more conservative in this age
of polarized American politics. One advantage of living on the political
margins, however, is that it is easier to look around and judge exactly
who is on your side. As we have seen, compared to other Republican
primary voters, moderates and liberals hold a distinctive set of values
and priorities. Most tellingly, they are likely to be most clearly opposed
to the notion that religion should play a role in government policy.

Liberals and moderates: finding a champion

Thus far, we have demonstrated that liberals and moderates maintain a
distinctive profile in the universe of Republican presidential primary voters,
based on their party identification (or relative lack thereof); their secularism; their disagreement on abortion, a historically important issue to
Republican primary voters; their preferences for a candidate with a particular set of personal qualities; and their issue priorities. We now examine how
early, and how strongly, this bloc of voters united behind a single candidate

DOI: 10.1057/9781137577535.0007

in the Republican primaries of 2000, 2008, and 2012. Did this bloc of voters remain faithful to a candidate even when his chances at the nomination appeared to be in decline? Or did they succumb to momentum, abandoning their champion and bandwagoning with the likely nominee?

The 2000 nomination contest: John McCain, the moderate maverick

Few Republican presidential candidates owe so much to one performance in one primary as McCain. When the Arizona senator began his campaign in 1999, he was squarely situated in the second tier of candidates. George W. Bush, son of the former president and inheritor of the family's fundraising network, rapidly had become the favorite of the party establishment. Bush's main competition among more moderate Republicans appeared to be former Tennessee governor Lamar Alexander (who had run in 1996) and Elizabeth Dole (wife of Bob Dole, the 1996 Republican nominee). Both those candidates, however, bowed out months before the Iowa caucuses, ceding the race to Bush. McCain himself refused to compete in the Iowa caucuses, claiming that his opposition to ethanol subsidies (a popular policy in the farm state) made him persona non grata in a state so dependent on agriculture. Instead, he set up camp in New Hampshire, holding dozens of "town hall" meetings in which he answered voters' questions. He depicted himself as a reformer: His campaign bus was dubbed "The Straight Talk Express," and he held a joint event with Democratic presidential candidate Bill Bradley to tout campaign finance reform. (He later succeeded in passing campaign finance reform legislation with Wisconsin Democrat Russ Feingold during Bush's first term.) He emphasized balancing the federal budget, while Bush advocated for tax cuts.

McCain's qualities and issue positions were, in fact, an archetype of what moderate GOP primary voters like.[2] While he was a Christian, he did not broadcast it or apply any type of political import to his faith. Indeed, later in the campaign he specifically attacked Pat Robertson, a leading evangelical conservative. McCain was also pro-life but said little about his stance. In a field whose front runner said in a debate that his favorite political philosopher was Jesus Christ, McCain stood out as the most secular alternative.

Finally, his bold, "truth teller" persona highlighted the type of candidate who excites moderates. He was someone for whom partisan labels were a suit of convenience, not a straightjacket, and his mesh of

DOI: 10.1057/9781137577535.0007

conservative and liberal ideas told both party's bases things they did not want to hear. Moderates loved it, however, as it echoed their sense that they were rational people looking out for the common good in the face of loud and more emotionally, ideologically driven agendas.

The New Hampshire primary electorate was an audience tailor-made for the Arizona senator. The primary is an open contest, in which voters who are registered "undeclared" (without a party affiliation) may vote in either party's election. Undeclared voters are often confused with independents, but in fact many lean toward one party or the other. Nevertheless, this group of voters does tend to be more moderate than declared Republicans. In addition, New Hampshire Republicans tend to be more moderate than their peers in other states, and social conservatives wield much less influence there than elsewhere. Even after skipping Iowa, McCain scored a surprising double-digit percentage victory in New Hampshire a week later, on the strength of his standing among moderates and liberals. He won a clear majority of those voters, who comprised 49 percent of the electorate.

As the field narrowed after New Hampshire, moderate and liberal Republican voters gravitated toward McCain (Figure 2.2). For example,

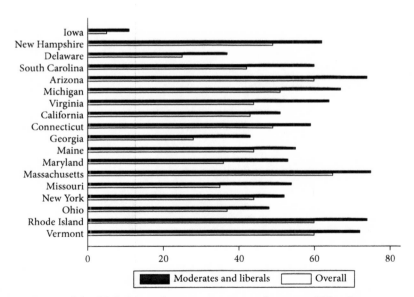

FIGURE 2.2   *John McCain's performance among moderates and liberals, 2000*
Source: Weighted exit poll data, 2000.

DOI: 10.1057/9781137577535.0007

in South Carolina, where McCain suffered a decisive defeat to Bush, he nonetheless performed just as well among the liberal and moderate voters in that Southern state as he had in New Hampshire. In the contests that followed, McCain always performed best among liberal and moderate voters, compared to more conservative ones. In 14 of 16 post–New Hampshire contests with exit polls, McCain won a plurality or majority of moderate and liberal voters, even though McCain lost most of these states to Bush (Table 2.2).

To determine whether the ideology of Republican primary voters was a significant factor in their choice of candidate (controlling for other potentially important factors) after the field was winnowed down, we ran a multivariate logistic regression of the McCain vote in the 14 contests after South Carolina in which exit polling took place (McCain withdrew from the race March 9). Other factors we considered besides ideology included demographic variables such as the age of the voter, gender, income, and education level; membership in the "Religious Right," a movement of religious conservatives within the Republican Party; and whether the primary took place in the South. We also

TABLE 2.2   *Candidate performance among moderate and liberal voters, 2000*

Primary/caucus	Date	Bush	Forbes	Keyes	McCain
Iowa (caucus)	January 24	45	33	6	11
New Hampshire	February 1	26	10	2	62
Delaware	February 8	45	16	1	37
South Carolina	February 19	36	*	3	60
Arizona	February 22	23	*	2	74
Michigan	February 22	29	*	2	67
Virginia	February 29	33	*	2	64
California	March 7	48	*	1	51
Connecticut	March 7	37	*	2	59
Georgia	March 7	56	*	1	43
Maine	March 7	40	*	2	55
Maryland	March 7	42	*	5	53
Massachusetts	March 7	23	*	1	75
Missouri	March 7	43	*	3	54
New York	March 7	43	*	4	52
Ohio	March 7	48	*	2	48
Rhode Island	March 7	25	*	1	74
Vermont	March 7	26	*	1	72

* withdrew from race
Source: Weighted exit poll data, 2000.

DOI: 10.1057/9781137577535.0007

controlled for the "favorite son" effect when the primary took place in the candidate's home state.

Our analysis indicates that even after controlling for these other variables, a voter's ideology remained a significant factor in vote choice. The more moderate a voter's ideology, the more likely that voter was to cast a vote for McCain; the more conservative a voter's ideology, the less likely. A voter's age and income were insignificant factors. Male voters were more likely to vote for McCain than female voters. The more educated a voter, the more likely the voter was to support McCain. McCain performed worse among Southerners, and among "religious right" voters. He did better among primary voters who did not identify themselves as Republicans, such as independents (Table 2.3).

TABLE 2.3   *Logistic regression analysis of McCain's vote in 2000, post-South Carolina*

VARIABLES	Vote for McCain
Male	0.16[...]
	(3.85)
Age	0.03
	(1.20)
Income	0.01
	(0.63)
Education	0.12[...]
	(5.74)
Religious Right	-0.75[...]
	(-13.13)
Republican	-1.12[...]
	(-25.85)
South	-0.37[...]
	(-7.54)
McCain Home State	1.00[...]
	(14.03)
Conservatism	-0.69[...]
	(-22.26)
Constant	1.23[...]
	(10.69)
N	16,058

t statistics in parentheses

* $p < 0.05$, ** $p < 0.01$, *** $p < 0.001$

Source: Pooled and weighted exit poll data from primaries, 2000.

DOI: 10.1057/9781137577535.0007

The 2008 nomination contest: The maverick returns

McCain began 2007 as the putative frontrunner for the Republican nomination. But by summer, he was bereft of all the accoutrements of a top-tier campaign: woefully short on money, he cut staff, and showed up virtually alone in his second political home, New Hampshire. One thing the Arizona senator had not lost, however, was his attractiveness to moderate and liberal Republican primary voters. This was true not just in New Hampshire, but across the nation.

In December 2007, former New York City mayor Rudy Giuliani led the field with 26 percent in the final Gallup survey of the year, taken just a few weeks before Iowans caucused. No other candidate could claim even 20 percent of Republican voters (Figure 2.3) in an unsettled field. For instance, although Giuliani led in national polls, his campaign was a virtual nonentity in Iowa. Emulating McCain's 2000 strategy, the socially moderate New York Republican had written off Iowa and its social conservatives as a poor fit for his candidacy. But in a puzzling twist, Giuliani had all but abandoned competing in New Hampshire by December 2007 in favor of the Florida primary three weeks after the Granite State. In retrospect, one might consider Giuliani's "lead" in national polls as the residue of widespread name recognition as "America's Mayor" after the events of September 11, 2001.

Although no clear national frontrunner had emerged by the end of the "invisible primary" portion of the nomination season, Republican voters had learned significant things about the candidates composing the field. They also had made important, lasting judgments about which candidates would be acceptable nominees, and as importantly, which candidates would not be acceptable.

Consider, for example, the results of the Gallup poll when respondents' ideology is taken into account. Giuliani's support varied significantly by the ideology of the respondent, from 48 percent of liberals to 35 percent of moderates to just 20 percent of self-identified conservatives. In contrast, the candidates in second and third place in the Gallup poll depended mostly on conservatives' support for their national standing. Former Tennessee senator Fred Thompson, at 18 percent nationally, scored 19 percent among conservatives, but possessed only single-digit support among moderates and liberals. Similarly, former Arkansas governor Mike Huckabee enjoyed 22 percent support among conservatives, but barely registered among moderates and liberals. The trend continued with McCain, whose ideological base mirrored Giuliani's; and former

DOI: 10.1057/9781137577535.0007

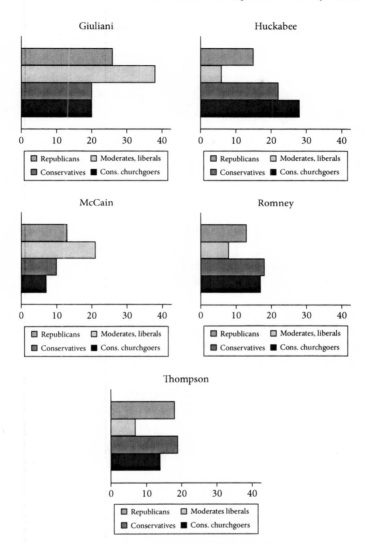

FIGURE 2.3 *Preference for Republican nomination, December 2007*
Source: Gallup poll of national Republican primary voters, December 14-16, 2007.

Massachusetts governor Mitt Romney, whose support profile resembled Thompson's and Huckabee's, despite the concerns of social conservatives about his late conversion to their point of view on issues such as banning abortion.

DOI: 10.1057/9781137577535.0007

Thus, just a few weeks before primaries and caucuses began, neither of the best-known names in the field, the "moderate" candidates Giuliani and McCain, displayed much crossover potential to conservatives. And no candidate favored mainly by conservatives had succeeded in gathering a large portion of the dominant ideological base of the GOP. A key reason behind the disunity of conservatives was the divisions among churchgoing conservatives. Among those voters, the poorly funded Huckabee was the most popular, outshining the much better known Giuliani and McCain, as well as others vying for the conservative mantle such as Romney and Thompson.

Republican voters' ability to sort out the various contenders for their party's nomination, and identify with a particular candidate as the banner-carrier for their particular ideology, also displayed itself in terms of their stated approval or disapproval of the various candidates. Once upon a time in presidential nomination seasons, a little-known candidate had to hope to gain national recognition after the actual contests started, by performing better than expected in Iowa and New Hampshire. But in 2008, what was striking was the degree to which the major candidates were all fairly well-known commodities, inasmuch as voters felt comfortable in making some sort of judgment about them. Even the lightly funded Huckabee, the least well-known of the five, was recognized to this extent by six of ten voters. One step above Huckabee was Romney and Thompson, who were recognized by 66 and 70 percent of those surveyed, respectively. And finally, Giuliani and McCain, the two candidates who entered the race with national recognition, had roughly nine of ten surveyed willing to make a rudimentary judgment about them.

The ideology of those surveyed once again appeared to have an impact on whether they looked favorably or unfavorably on a particular candidate. Only Giuliani appeared to have broad-based support, appealing to conservative Republicans (+ 49 net favorable) and moderate/liberal Republicans (+ 48 net favorable) in equal measure. In contrast, McCain, Giuliani's counterpart of equal stature, was almost twice as likely to be approved by moderate/liberal Republicans (+ 56 net favorable) than conservative Republicans (+ 33 net favorable). Conversely, the three candidates who drew their support predominantly from conservatives, Huckabee, Romney, and Thompson, all possessed much higher net favorables among those voters than among moderate and liberal Republicans.

DOI: 10.1057/9781137577535.0007

One last measure of the degree of coherence and consistency of Republican voters' opinions, on the eve of Iowa and New Hampshire, can be seen in the results of Gallup's query as to respondents' "second choice" for the GOP nomination. Throughout the pre-primary period, Giuliani and McCain had continually been highlighted as candidates with an issue-profile that was distinctive in some respects from the conventional conservative views of the party. Indeed, the two candidates made no secret of their mutual respect for each other. Perhaps unsurprisingly then, many Giuliani supporters had absorbed enough cues to recognize McCain as a suitable substitute for their first choice. McCain, Romney, and Thompson supporters all listed Giuliani as their second choice in roughly equal percentages. Supporters of Huckabee, whose most prominent characteristic was his social conservatism, were much less likely to list Giuliani as a second choice.

The results of the first caucuses and primaries confirmed the continued adherence of moderate and liberal Republican voters to McCain, eight years after he broke onto the national political scene with his victory in New Hampshire. In Iowa, a state McCain ignored in 2000 and spent far less time there in 2008 than Huckabee or Romney, the Arizona senator finished fourth with 13 percent, just behind Thompson. Among moderate and liberal caucus-goers, however, McCain finished virtually tied for first with Romney, carrying a quarter of those voters.

Not far behind McCain and Romney among moderate and liberal Republican primary voters was Texas congressman Ron Paul. Although lionized among libertarians,[3] he had a quite low national profile when he strode onto a South Carolina stage in May 2007 to participate in the second debate of the Republican nomination season. A Fox News correspondent identified him as the only candidate who opposed the war in Iraq and supported almost immediate withdrawal of U. S. forces. He then asked, "Are you out of step with your party? Is your party out of step with the rest of the world? If either of those is the case, why are you seeking its nomination?"

Paul responded,

> Well, I think the party has lost its way, because the conservative wing of the Republican Party always advocated a noninterventionist foreign policy... There's a strong tradition of being anti-war in the Republican party. It is the constitutional position. It is the advice of the Founders to follow a non-interventionist foreign policy, stay out of entangling alliances, be friends with countries, negotiate and talk with them and trade with them.[4]

DOI: 10.1057/9781137577535.0007

When asked whether the September 11 attacks had changed that Republican tradition, Paul replied that U.S. intervention in the Middle East had prompted 9/11 ("Have you ever read the reasons they attacked us? They attack us because we've been over there; we've been bombing Iraq for 10 years"). Paul's response drew the ire of Rudy Giuliani, who called upon Paul to retract his "extraordinary" statement. Paul proceeded to double down: "If we think that we can do what we want around the world and not incite hatred, then we have a problem. They don't come here to attack us because we're rich and we're free. They come and they attack us because we're over there. I mean, what would we think if we were—if other foreign countries were doing that to us?"

In the 2008 Iowa caucuses, Paul finished fifth with 10 percent, but carried nearly twice that amount among moderate and liberal voters. This bloc had a unique profile among Republican primary voters: very few said terrorism was a major issue, while many expressed concern about American involvement in Iraq.

Days later in New Hampshire, his adopted second political home, McCain not only gained a needed victory in order to advance to the later rounds of the nomination battle. He cemented himself as the champion of moderate and liberal voters. In the Granite State, McCain defeated Romney by just 5 percentage points statewide. But among liberal and moderate voters, the Arizona senator won nearly half the vote, nearly doubling Romney and far outshining Giuliani. The former mayor had largely abandoned New Hampshire in the closing weeks, putting all his hopes into winning the state of Florida, held three weeks after New Hampshire. Giuliani was correct that the Sunshine State's Republican electorate was a good match for a moderate candidate; what his campaign failed to understand was that moderate and liberal voters already had found their champion in the New Hampshire victor, and were unwilling to reconsider. In almost every contest on February 5, McCain finished with either a strong plurality or outright majority among moderate and liberal voters (Figure 2.4). (The only exceptions were in the Nevada caucuses and Utah primary, where Romney enjoyed the support of a large contingent of Mormon voters; and Arkansas, where Huckabee had a favorite-son advantage.) After Romney dropped out of the race February 7, McCain's dominance among these voters became even more pronounced. He carried 60 percent or more of moderate and liberal voters in Maryland, Ohio, Vermont, Virginia, and Wisconsin (Table 2.4).

DOI: 10.1057/9781137577535.0007

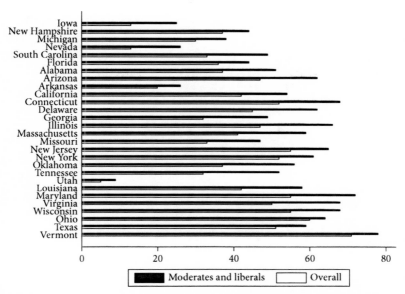

FIGURE 2.4 *McCain's relative performance among moderates and liberals, 2008.*
Source: Weighted exit poll data, 2008.

To determine whether the ideology of Republican primary voters was a significant factor in their choice of candidate (controlling for other potentially important factors) after the field was winnowed down, we ran a multivariate logistic regression of the McCain vote in the 16 contests after Nevada and South Carolina, through February 5, in which exit polling took place (Romney dropped out of the contest February 7). Other factors we considered besides ideology included demographic variables such as the age of the voter, gender, income, and education level; whether a voter described himself as born-again; whether a voter identified as a member of the Republican Party; and whether the primary took place in the South. We also controlled for the "favorite son" effect when a primary took place in a candidate's home state (Table 2.5).

Our analysis indicates that even after controlling for a host of demographic variables, a voter's ideology remained a significant factor in choosing McCain. Older and higher-income voters were more likely to vote for McCain. Male voters were more likely to choose McCain than female voters. McCain tended to perform worse among evangelicals. Unlike 2000, self-identified Republicans were more likely to choose McCain than non-Republicans. But just as in 2000, the more

TABLE 2.4   *Candidate performance among moderate and liberal voters, 2008*

Primary/caucus	Date	Huckabee	McCain	Romney
Iowa (caucus)	January 3	20	25	25
New Hampshire	January 8	11	44	24
Michigan	January 15	11	38	33
South Carolina	January 19	21	49	11
Nevada (caucus)	January 19	8	26	35
Florida	January 29	8	44	22
Alabama	February 5	31	51	12
Arizona	February 5	6	62	18
Arkansas	February 5	62	26	5
California	February 5	9	54	21
Connecticut	February 5	4	68	15
Delaware	February 5	6	62	23
Georgia	February 5	26	49	19
Illinois	February 5	7	66	19
Massachusetts	February 5	4	59	32
Missouri	February 5	19	47	25
New Jersey	February 5	6	65	14
New York	February 5	8	61	18
Oklahoma	February 5	20	56	17
Tennessee	February 5	24	52	10
Utah	February 5	1	9	85
Louisiana	February 9	27	58	*
Maryland	February 12	18	72	*
Virginia	February 12	24	68	*
Wisconsin	February 19	24	68	*
Ohio	March 4	23	64	*
Texas	March 4	25	59	*
Vermont	March 4	9	78	*

* withdrew from race.
Source: Weighted exit poll data, 2008.

conservative the voter, the less likely he would choose McCain, controlling for other factors.

The 2012 nomination contest: McCain and Romney, brothers in moderation

In January 2012, McCain traveled to New Hampshire, not to make a third run for the presidency, but to endorse Romney, who was attempting once again to earn his party's nomination. At first glance, McCain and Romney were an unlikely pairing. McCain had made no secret of his disdain for Romney during the 2008 contest. But in another sense, it was a passing of

TABLE 2.5 *Logistic regression of McCain vote in 2008, post-South Carolina*

VARIABLES	Vote for McCain
Male	0.15**
	(3.14)
Age	0.20***
	(8.04)
Education	0.01
	(0.28)
Income	0.04**
	(2.87)
Evangelical	−0.28***
	(−5.38)
Population Density	−0.04
	(−1.10)
South	−0.10
	(−1.74)
Republican	0.23***
	(4.18)
Conservatism	−0.76***
	(−23.79)
Huckabee Home State	−0.71***
	(−6.77)
Romney Home State	−0.11
	(−1.09)
McCain Home State	0.35***
	(3.97)
Constant	0.12
	(0.78)
N	11,501

t statistics in parentheses
* $p < 0.05$, ** $p < 0.01$, *** $p < 0.001$
Source: Pooled and weighted exit poll data, 2008.

the torch: for the second consecutive cycle, the favorite of the moderate/liberal faction of the Republican Party was primed to be the nominee.

Just like McCain, Romney was able to count on a strong performance among moderates and liberals to offset weakness among more conservative Republican voters. In Iowa, he attracted a third of moderates and liberals, nearly doubling his statewide performance. He won similar levels of support in states friendly (New Hampshire) and unfriendly (South Carolina) to him.

DOI: 10.1057/9781137577535.0007

In the early states, Romney had competition for these voters from a seemingly unlikely source: Ron Paul, who also was making his second run for the Republican nomination, continued his success among moderates and liberals. In Iowa, where he finished third overall, he led all candidates among liberal and moderate voters, carrying four of ten. Paul's popularity carried into New Hampshire, where he finished second overall, and second to Romney among liberal and moderate voters with a quarter of the vote. Paul's numbers quickly declined, however, in subsequent contests. He was especially unpopular in southern states, even among liberal and moderate voters. (One exception to this was Virginia, where he was the only alternative to Romney on the ballot, thanks to the failure of other candidates to meet ballot inclusion requirements.) Paul's failure in the South was perhaps due to one of the sources of his strength elsewhere, his opposition to American military involvement in Iraq and Afghanistan. The South has traditionally been America's most hawkish region, and even Southern moderates are likely to share some of their region's beliefs.

Paul's support came from a distinct section of the moderate faction, independents under the age of 35.[5] State exit polls consistently showed Paul doing best in almost linear fashion among the young, the independent, and the moderate. It stands to reason that younger, moderate voters without strong partisan attachments found him attractive, especially since the younger a voter is the likelier he or she is to have come of political age when the dominant foreign policy issues were Iraq and America's military response to the September 11 attacks.

Another competitor for the moderate-liberal bloc was Jon Huntsman, the former governor of Utah who had joined the Obama administration as the U.S. Ambassador to China. Huntsman, who ignored Iowa and focused on New Hampshire only to finish third there, became a case study in the difficulty of building a winning Republican nomination coalition from a base comprised of moderates and liberals. He departed the race before the South Carolina primary.

Huntsman's campaign suffered from a muddled message. Those parts which were clear emphasized issues such as his belief in climate change, which have not historically resonated with GOP moderates. While Paul could appeal as a strong truth-teller in opposition to both party's bases, Huntsman avoided displaying the strong temperament to which moderate Republicans are typically attracted. He also quietly backed party economic orthodoxy on tax cuts rather than, like McCain in 2000,

DOI: 10.1057/9781137577535.0007

favoring balanced budgets and government economy rather than further revenue-losing tax cuts. As such, Huntsman had limited appeal to the more traditional GOP moderate and instead found himself most popular among the very few liberals voting in the New Hampshire primary. Indeed, Huntsman won pluralities among only four groups of voters in the New Hampshire exit poll: self-described Democrats, Tea Party opponents, those dissatisfied with the entire GOP field, and those satisfied with Obama. Small wonder, then, that his voter appeal was limited despite his seeming moderation.

Romney, on the other hand, was for the typical McCain moderate the best alternative among an unappealing bunch. His Mormonism meant he was often opposed by the evangelical Christians whom moderates find so undesirable, and he clearly soft-pedaled any strong position on social issues. Many New Hampshire residents surely remembered his quite moderate tenure as governor of neighboring Massachusetts, and he projected experience and stability to all groups of voters. Had Huntsman's campaign been more moderate and less liberal, he might have been able to challenge Romney for leadership of this group. As the field stood on

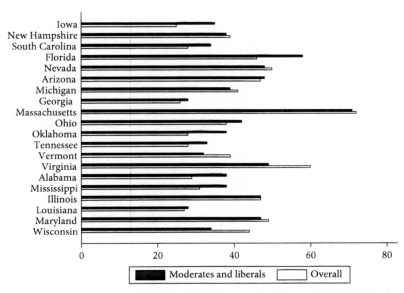

FIGURE 2.5   *Mitt Romney's relative performance among moderates and liberals, 2012*

Source: Weighted exit poll data, 2012.

DOI: 10.1057/9781137577535.0007

New Hampshire primary eve, however, Romney was the most acceptable candidate available to mainstream moderate Republicans.

Weeks later, in the decisive state of Florida, Romney enjoyed dominance, carrying an outright majority of moderates and liberals and defeating his chief rival Newt Gingrich among this faction by a 3-1 margin. In almost every subsequent state, Romney led among these voters (the exceptions were Gingrich's home state of Georgia; Virginia, where he split these voters with Paul almost evenly; and Louisiana) (Table 2.6).

To determine whether the ideology of Republican primary voters was a significant factor in their choice of candidate (controlling for other potentially important factors) after the field was winnowed down, we ran a multivariate logistic regression of the Romney vote in the 16 contests after Florida in which exit polling took place. Other factors we considered besides ideology included demographic variables such as the age of the voter, gender, income, and education level; whether a voter described himself as born-again; whether a voter identified as a member of the Republican Party; the population density of the voter's area of

TABLE 2.6   *Candidate performance among moderate and liberal voters, 2012*

Primary/caucus	Date	Gingrich	Romney	Santorum
Iowa (caucus)	January 3	6	35	8
New Hampshire	January 10	3	38	5
South Carolina	January 21	31	34	13
Florida	January 31	20	58	7
Nevada (caucus)	February 4	12	48	4
Arizona	February 28	17	48	15
Michigan	February 28	6	39	33
Georgia	March 6	39	28	17
Massachusetts	March 6	4	71	9
Ohio	March 6	11	42	28
Oklahoma	March 6	27	38	19
Tennessee	March 6	21	33	28
Vermont	March 6	5	32	19
Virginia	March 6	*	49	*
Alabama	March 13	18	38	28
Mississippi	March 13	26	38	27
Illinois	March 20	7	47	26
Louisiana	March 24	14	28	39
Maryland	April 3	10	47	22
Wisconsin	April 3	7	34	32

*Did not qualify for the ballot.
Source: Weighted exit poll data, 2012.

DOI: 10.1057/9781137577535.0007

residence (i.e., urban, suburban, or rural); and whether the primary took place in the South. We also controlled for the "favorite son" effect when a primary took place in a candidate's home state.

Our analysis (Table 2.7) indicates that even after controlling for other factors, a voter's ideology remained a significant factor in vote choice. The more moderate a voter's ideology, the more likely that voter was to cast a vote for Romney. Older, wealthier, and better educated voters also were more likely to vote for Romney, as were self-identified Republicans. The gender of the voter was insignificant after controlling for other

TABLE 2.7   *Logistic regression of Romney vote in 2012, post-Florida*

VARIABLES	Vote for Romney
Male	−0.04
	(−1.08)
Age	0.28***
	(10.45)
Education	0.09***
	(4.28)
Income	0.16***
	(8.67)
Evangelical	−0.57***
	(−14.12)
Population Density	−0.11***
	(−4.04)
South	−0.45***
	(−11.26)
Republican	0.78***
	(16.44)
Conservatism	−0.23***
	(−9.46)
Romney Home State	1.13***
	(15.38)
Gingrich Home State	−0.31***
	(−4.63)
Constant	−1.34***
	(−9.17)
N	23,053

t statistics in parentheses
* $p < 0.05$, ** $p < 0.01$, *** $p < 0.001$
Source: Weighted and pooled exit poll data, 2012.

DOI: 10.1057/9781137577535.0007

factors. Evangelicals, southerners, and those who lived in rural areas were less likely to vote for Romney.

Conclusions

In this chapter, we have demonstrated that liberals and moderates display a distinctive profile in the universe of Republican presidential primary voters, based on their party identification (or relative lack thereof); their secularism; their disagreement on abortion, a historically important issue to Republican primary voters; their preferences for a candidate with a particular set of personal qualities, including independence of mind; and their issue priorities. We also have shown how this bloc of voters united early behind a single candidate in the Republican primaries of 2000, 2008, and 2012. The Republican Party's primaries are often said to be dominated by the far right, but it was the moderates' choice who won the nomination in 2008 and 2012. The reason their choice did not win in 2000 is due to the characteristics and preferences of the GOP's largest faction, the somewhat conservatives.

Notes

1   The 1996 New Hampshire exit poll showed Alexander received 33 percent of somewhat liberal voters (8 percent of the electorate) and 30 percent of the moderate voters (35 percent). Dole by comparison received 24 percent of the somewhat liberals and 26 percent of the moderates. Alexander also led Dole among Independents (35 percent of the electorate) by a 27-18 margin, and among Democrats (3 percent) by 34-14.

2   We find common ground here with Hagen et al. (2000), and Paolino and Shaw (2001).

3   Libertarianism is a philosophy that advocates for very minimal government interference in all aspects of a person's life. Thus, they tend to argue for the repeal of virtually all social insurance and welfare programs at all levels of government. They also argue against any form of business regulation of terms and conditions of employment such as the minimum wage and overtime laws. They also favor legalization of drugs, same-sex marriage, and Internet privacy. Falling as they do on both sides of the traditional left-right divide, it is not clear how they might answer the standard ideology question that only presents liberal, conservative, or moderate as the options. Paul

DOI: 10.1057/9781137577535.0007

consistently ran better among moderates in both 2008 and 2012 than he did among conservatives, suggesting a sizeable fraction of libertarians say they are moderate when presented with the standard ideological question. For a study of Paul as a third-party phenomenon, see Chamberlain (2010).

4 For a transcript, see http://www.nytimes.com/2007/05/15/us/ politics/16repubs-text.html?pagewanted=print&_r=0. Accessed October 20, 2015.

5 In New Hampshire, Paul won 46 percent of the 18–24 set and 35 percent of the 30–39 set. He won 29 percent of 40–49 year olds, 28 percent of 50–64 set, and only 12 percent of 65+ voters. He also won 31 percent of the Independents. In Iowa, Paul won 48 percent of voters between 18 and 29, 26 percent of voters 30–44, 16 percent between 50 and 64, and only 11 percent of 65+ voters. He won 43 percent of Independents.

DOI: 10.1057/9781137577535.0007

3
Somewhat Conservatives

Abstract: *This group is the most numerous nationally and in most states, comprising 35–40 percent of the national GOP electorate. While the numbers of moderates, very conservative and evangelical voters vary significantly by state, somewhat conservative voters are found in similar proportions in every state. They are not very vocal, but they form the bedrock base of the Republican Party. They also have a significant distinction: they always back the winner. The candidate who garners their favor has won each of the last four open races. These voters' preferred candidate profile can be inferred from the characteristics of their favored candidates: Bob Dole in 1996, George W. Bush in 2000, John McCain in 2008, and Mitt Romney in 2012. They like even-keeled men with substantial governing experience. They like people who express conservative values on the economy or social issues, but who do not espouse radical change.*

Keywords: conservatism; ideology; presidential elections; presidential primaries; Republican Party

Olsen, Henry, and Dante J. Scala. *The Four Faces of the Republican Party: The Fight for the 2016 Presidential Nomination.* New York: Palgrave Macmillan, 2015. DOI: 10.1057/9781137577535.0008.

DOI: 10.1057/9781137577535.0008

The most important Republican Party faction we discuss is the one most journalists do not understand and therefore ignore: somewhat conservative voters. This group is the most numerous nationally. In most states, it comprises 35–40 percent of the national GOP electorate. While the numbers of moderates, very conservative and evangelical voters vary significantly by state, somewhat conservative voters are found in similar proportions in every state. They are not very vocal, but they form the bedrock base of the Republican Party.

They also have a significant distinction: they always back the winner. The candidate who garners their favor has won each of the last four open presidential nomination contests. This tendency appears at the state level as well. Look at the exit polls from virtually any state caucus or primary since 1996, and you will find that the winner either led (or at least ran roughly even) among somewhat conservative voters.

These voters' preferred candidate profile can be inferred from the characteristics of their favored candidates: Bob Dole in 1996, George W. Bush in 2000, John McCain in 2008, and Mitt Romney in 2012. They like even-keeled men with substantial governing experience. They like people who express conservative values on the economy or social issues, but who do not espouse radical change. They like people who are optimistic about America; the somewhat conservative voter rejects "culture warriors" such as Pat Buchanan in the 1990s. They are conservative in both senses of the word: they prefer the ideals of American conservatism while displaying the cautious disposition of the Burkean who defaults to tradition above all else.

Somewhat conservatives are, to play on established images, like the stereotypical small- business person who is the prototypical Republican. They are not highly ideological; instead, they are practical people who want to get on with their generally comfortable lives without much inter-ference or denigration from elites. They do not like having their lives condemned, whether by economic populists running against economic-ally successful people or by progressives who think traditional American family life is oppressive. They are not libertarians in any serious sense of the word: they are perfectly satisfied to pay taxes for things they value and that seem to work for them, such as old age entitlements, decent public schools and universities, good roads, and public safety. They do, however, want to be "left alone" inasmuch as they do not think bureau-crats or other elites have their best interests at heart when they try to tax, regulate, or dominate them in the name of "public interest."

DOI: 10.1057/9781137577535.0008

In the current Republican Party, departing Speaker of the House John Boehner is probably the best-known archetype of these people. Decent, practical, deeply committed to free enterprise and traditional values, Boehner epitomizes the somewhat conservative demeanor and world view. His desire to create consensus rather than conflict, to do rather than to speak, could come straight out of the suburban or small-town Chamber of Commerce playbook. And when more ideological conservatives want change to come faster or more deeply, his calm, steady attempt to accommodate but not bend over backwards to adopt the more strident views of his fellow members is exactly how the somewhat conservative voter reacts to similarly styled candidates in primaries.

Fiscally and socially very conservative voters may view these voters as "establishment moderates," but this is neither how these voters see themselves nor how their stated viewpoints line up compared to real moderates. Instead, they are moderate only in comparison to more activist conservatives. In fact, one major reason these people remain conservative and Republican is precisely the activist immoderation they readily associate with what they see as liberal, big-government Democrats.

As such, somewhat conservative voters are best described as the sensible median voters of the Republican primary electorate. In their opinions and sentiments, they overlap each of the outlying segments of the Republican electorate—moderates and liberals to their left, very conservative voters to their right—in some fashion. Unlike their peers, they are not engaged in identity politics, nor are they trying to remake the party in their own image. Arguably, they are the party.

Presence in the primary electorate

Unlike moderates and liberals, and conservative evangelicals, "somewhat conservative" voters are distributed more or less evenly throughout the Republican primary electorate, regardless of region. As a bloc, these voters are rarely less than 30 percent of the electorate, and rarely exceed 40 percent. In 2000, they comprised less than 30 percent of these voters in just one state (Vermont, 29 percent), and only in Louisiana and Tennessee did they comprise more than 40 percent. From 2000 to 2012, somewhat conservative voters neither increased nor decreased significantly in the primary electorate, with the exception of some decreases in the deep South (Figure 3.1).

DOI: 10.1057/9781137577535.0008

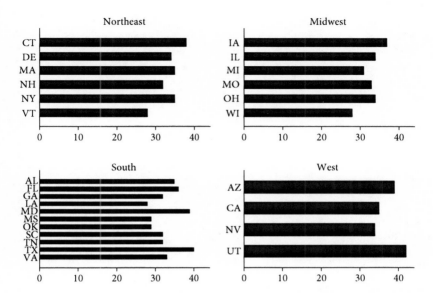

FIGURE 3.1 *Presence of somewhat conservative voters in Republican primaries and caucuses*

Source: Weighted exit poll data, 2008 and 2012.

Secularism

As a bloc, somewhat conservative voters tend to stand astride the divide between secular and religious voters within the Republican Party. In 2000, when the Religious Right was in its heyday, only about a quarter of somewhat conservatives said they considered themselves to be part of the conservative Christian movement, a small portion only slightly larger than the percentage of moderates and liberals who said so. Now, evangelical Christians comprise a significant minority of somewhat conservative voters, numbering roughly four of ten in 2008, and close to half in 2012. The presence of born-again Christians is significantly higher in this bloc than among moderates and liberals, but not dominant as they are among very conservative voters.

As a bloc, somewhat conservative voters are somewhat dutiful in their religious habits. In 2008, roughly half of these primary voters said they attend religious services once a week or more—a higher portion than among liberals and moderates, but not nearly as high as among very conservative voters (Table 3.1).

DOI: 10.1057/9781137577535.0008

TABLE 3.1   *Profile of somewhat conservative Republican voters*

		Somewhat conservatives	Other Republican primary voters
PARTY IDENTIFICATION			
Identify as Republican?	2008	80	72
	2012	73	66
TEA PARTY			
Support Tea Party	2012	64	59
ABORTION			
Should abortion be illegal in most or all cases?	2008	67	61
	2012	61	60
ISSUES			
Which issue mattered most in 2008?	Economy	41	39
	Illegal immigration	21	22
	War in Iraq	18	19
	Terrorism	17	16
Which issues mattered most in 2012?	Economy	58	54
	Deficit	29	27
	Abortion	7	10
CANDIDATE QUALITIES Which mattered most?			
2008	Shares my values	44	45
	Right experience	25	21
	Says what he believes	23	24
2012	Can defeat Obama	44	37
	Right experience	22	20
	Strong moral character	19	22
	True conservative	13	17

Source: Pooled and weighted exit poll data, 2008 and 2012. N. B.: Total number of respondents in 2008: 25,973; in 2012: 38,010. The number of respondents for each question, however, did vary.

When asked whether it mattered that a candidate share his religious beliefs, a majority of somewhat conservative voters consistently asserted that it was significant to them. In 2008 and 2012, more than 60 percent of this bloc said that sharing religious beliefs with a candidate mattered at least somewhat, if not a great deal. This was a larger percentage than among liberals and moderates, although not nearly as high as among very conservative voters.

DOI: 10.1057/9781137577535.0008

Abortion

On the question of abortion, somewhat conservative voters occupied a middle ground: wary of abortion on demand, but reluctant to support the prohibition favored by very conservative evangelicals. In 2000, just one of seven somewhat conservative voters said abortion should be outlawed completely—a small minority similar to that of moderates and liberals, as opposed to the nearly one-half of Religious Right voters who supported an outright ban. On the other hand, almost all of somewhat conservatives were uncomfortable with abortion on demand, a stance that put them closer to very conservative voters than their liberal and moderate counterparts. A plurality of somewhat conservatives expressed support for a middle ground on the issue, albeit one tilted toward more restrictions on abortion rather than fewer. This pattern persisted in 2008 and 2012. Although somewhat conservative voters tended to favor restrictions on abortion, they were very unlikely to list abortion as a crucial issue. In 2000, fewer than one out of ten of these voters said abortion mattered most when deciding how they voted in the primary. Twelve years later, this percentage remained virtually identical.

Issue priorities

In the 2000 primaries, exit pollsters asked Republican primary voters whether "moral values" was an issue that mattered most to their voting decisions – an apparent reference to Bill Clinton's misdeeds during his time in the White House. A plurality of somewhat conservative voters said "moral values" was the issue that mattered most in their voting decisions—a percentage similar to that of very conservative voters.

Somewhat conservatives were also between the two Republican poles on fiscal issues in 2000. They were more likely than moderates and liberals to list taxes as their most important issue, and less likely to list Social Security. As we will see, their priorities mirrored Bush's, not McCain's, in this respect.

In the 2008 primaries, a large plurality of somewhat conservatives said the economy was the most important issue facing the country. On all four issues offered to voters as options (illegal immigration, the

DOI: 10.1057/9781137577535.0008

war in Iraq, the economy, and terrorism), the percentage of somewhat conservatives who said it was most important always fell between the percentage of moderates and liberals who cited it as most important, and the percentage of very conservative voters who did so.

In 2012, somewhat conservative primary voters, like their peers, were mainly focused on the economy and the federal budget as the key issues of the primaries. Roughly six of ten said the economy mattered most in their vote choice, a percentage closer to the portion of moderates and liberals who said so. Three of ten said the deficit was their key issue—a percentage that more closely resembled their very conservative peers.

Candidate qualities

In 2012, when asked what candidate quality mattered most in deciding how they would vote, a near-majority of somewhat conservative Republicans cited the ability to defeat Barack Obama. Roughly two of ten pointed to "the right experience," and another two of ten chose "strong moral character." The least-chosen answer was a candidate who was a "true conservative."

In 2008, nearly a majority of somewhat conservative voters said that the candidate quality that mattered most was that the candidate share the voter's values. This was a higher percentage than among moderates and liberals, but not nearly as high as among very conservative evangelicals. Once again, somewhat conservative voters were more likely to cite candidate experience and willingness to speak one's beliefs than their more conservative counterparts, but not as likely as moderates and liberals.

In 2000, when confronted with seven choices, roughly one of four somewhat conservative voters said the candidate quality that mattered most in their voting decision was the candidate's ability to stand up for his beliefs. This was a higher percentage than among very conservative voters, but not nearly as high as among moderates and liberals. Another quarter of somewhat conservative voters said that a candidate who represents conservative values was most important—a significantly higher percentage than among moderates and liberals, but far less than among very conservative voters.

DOI: 10.1057/9781137577535.0008

Party identification

Most somewhat conservative voters identify themselves as Republicans, though a not insignificant portion describe themselves as independent of party affiliation. Three-quarters of these voters described themselves as Republicans in 2000, while two of ten said they were independents. The percentage of self-described Republicans remained roughly similar in 2008 and 2012.

In reaction to the Tea Party movement that sprung up after the 2008 elections, a majority of this bloc was supportive, though not in the near-unanimity that greeted the Tea Party among very conservative voters. About a third of somewhat conservative voters said they were either neutral or opposed to the movement—far more ambivalent than their very conservative peers, but far less so than moderate and liberal Republican primary voters. Even that support tended to be even keeled. A 2011 *Wall Street Journal / NBC News* poll (March 31 - April 4) found that half of all Republicans who supported the Tea Party described themselves as Republicans first; the other half said they were Tea Partiers first. Given what we know about the distinction between very conservative voters and somewhat conservative voters, it is likely that well over a majority of somewhat conservative Tea Party supporters thought of themselves as Republicans first while a strong majority of very conservative voters said the opposite.

The quiet resistance of somewhat conservative voters to radical change within their party has manifested itself in recent nomination cycles. Invariably, we find that one of the early winners is someone who draws significant support from this group. As the race progresses and candidates drop out, we see the more established, less dynamic candidate picking up larger shares of the somewhat conservative vote compared to the more ideological, "change agent" candidate who inevitably emerges—from the left or the right—as the "boring candidate's" primary rival.

The 2000 nomination contest: Bush dominates

When the 2000 Republican nomination fight started in 1999, eventual nominee George W. Bush faced many potential competitors for somewhat conservative voters. Former Vice President Dan Quayle,

DOI: 10.1057/9781137577535.0008

former Transportation and Labor Secretary Elizabeth Dole, and former Governor and Education Secretary Lamar Alexander all had the mix of conservative views and governing experience that the party bedrock tends to like. Each had significant weaknesses, however, especially the fact that each had either lost their most recent race (Quayle, Alexander) or had never run for elected office at all (Dole). Bush had the benefit of winning two straight races in Texas, which in the 1990s was only in the process of moving from an ancestrally Democratic, albeit conservative state to the conservative GOP bastion it is today. With a solid governing and political track record behind him, it proved surprisingly easy for Bush to clear the somewhat conservative field of serious competition during the invisible primary, before actual contests began. All three potential rivals had exited the race by August, leaving Bush alone as the mature Republican with stature.

Once caucuses and primaries began in 2000, Bush led among somewhat conservatives from the outset (Figure 3.2). In Iowa, he won a near-majority of somewhat conservative voters, well above the 41 percent he received statewide. His hold on these voters (as well as those in other groups) faltered in New Hampshire to McCain, but he quickly

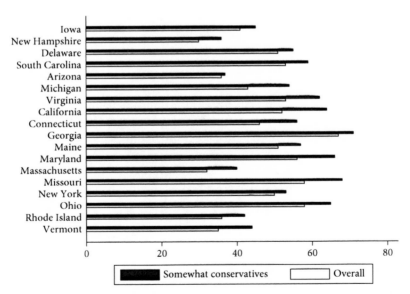

FIGURE 3.2   *George W. Bush's relative performance among somewhat conservative voters, 2000*

Source: Weighted exit poll data, 2000.

DOI: 10.1057/9781137577535.0008

regained dominance. Bush won 55 percent of somewhat conservative voters in Delaware, knocking Steve Forbes out of the race. He then carried 59 percent of somewhat conservative voters in the key state of South Carolina, allowing him to beat McCain in that crucial state by a comfortable margin. After South Carolina, Bush proceeded to dominate among these voters in most primaries. He carried 54 percent of somewhat conservatives in Michigan even while losing statewide because of the large number of self-proclaimed Democrats crossing over to vote for McCain. He rode a 62-35 margin among them in Virginia to a 9-point statewide victory, this time overcoming record high, pro-McCain turnouts in the more moderate DC suburbs. On March 7, the last day of primaries before McCain dropped out of the race, Bush lost this group of voters only in the very moderate New England states of Massachusetts, Rhode Island, and Vermont (Table 3.2).

While Bush fit the somewhat conservative prototype in 2000, the pattern observed in this race held true later in the decade as well. In particular, somewhat conservative voters tend to lean toward the dominant faction in any given state. The more moderates there are as a share of the total electorate, the more somewhat conservatives tend to

TABLE 3.2   *Candidate performance among somewhat conservative voters, 2000*

Primary/caucus	Date	Bush	Forbes	Keyes	McCain
Iowa (caucus)	January 24	45	32	10	4
New Hampshire	February 1	36	13	6	44
Delaware	February 8	55	21	2	22
South Carolina	February 19	59	*	4	37
Arizona	February 22	37	*	3	59
Michigan	February 22	54	*	7	39
Virginia	February 29	62	*	3	35
California	March 7	64	*	3	32
Connecticut	March 7	56	*	4	40
Georgia	March 7	71	*	4	25
Maine	March 7	57	*	1	41
Maryland	March 7	66	*	4	30
Massachusetts	March 7	40	*	4	55
Missouri	March 7	68	*	6	24
New York	March 7	53	*	2	43
Ohio	March 7	65	*	4	30
Rhode Island	March 7	42	*	4	54
Vermont	March 7	44	*	4	50

*Withdrew from the race.
Source: Weighted exit poll data, 2000.

DOI: 10.1057/9781137577535.0008

support moderate-supported candidates. Conversely, somewhat conservative voters tend to support religiously oriented candidates in greater numbers in states with large numbers of very conservative evangelicals. This pattern was particularly in evidence in 2008.

The 2008 nomination contest: McCain the statesman

The 2008 nomination contest started without an obvious establishment candidate. McCain had some claims on this group as a long-standing senator, but faced claims he was too much of a maverick (temperamentally and politically) to be the nominee. Perhaps his noticeable attempt to be a calm, reassuring presence in 2007 was calculated to appeal to these voters. Whether it was so or not, that and his lack of emphasis on non-Republican issues such as climate change and campaign finance in favor of a focus on foreign policy meant that by year's end he was viewed much more seriously by these voters than he was in 1999.

He faced three potential competitors for these voters. New York Mayor Rudy Giuliani, aka "America's Mayor," started the year in the lead among national polls. He, too, noticeably calmed down his "Noo Yawk" style of campaigning to run a national race. But he faced two problems McCain did not. He was openly pro-choice on abortion and sympathetic to gay rights as well. On fiscal issues, as mayor of New York City, he had opposed cuts in commuter income taxes imposed by the state and promoted municipal budgets with large spending increases. He might have fit the somewhat conservative preference for calm statesmen, but he was clearly to McCain's left on key conservative concerns.

Romney and Tennessee Senator Fred Thompson could also have laid claim to these voters, but both spent the year battling for the support of the very conservative fiscal set. When Thompson campaigned (his lackadaisical effort was much criticized by his supporters), he also tended to have a less distinguished and more populist approach than typically favored by somewhat conservative voters. Thus, somewhat conservative voters outside the evangelical community in the early contests tended to see McCain and Romney as their two potential choices. Giuliani and Thompson had faded such that neither man received over 15 percent of somewhat conservative votes in any of the races they contested.

But an unexpected candidate rose to challenge these two in the evangelical community, former Arkansas Governor Mike Huckabee. While

DOI: 10.1057/9781137577535.0008

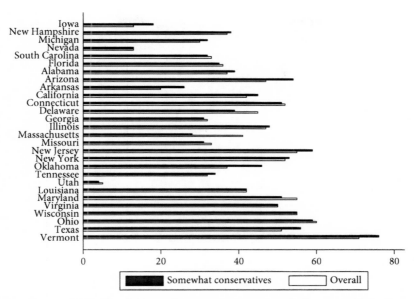

FIGURE 3.3 *McCain's relative performance among somewhat conservative voters,*
2008

Source: Weighted exit poll data, 2008.

his folksy and populist manner was not what these voters usually like, in
the South and among Iowa evangelicals a large number supported him
anyway. Thus, within the first few contests one could observe the factors
at play that ended up dominating the middle stage of the race and forcing
Romney from the contest.

Viewing the remaining contests through chronological and regional
lenses aids in the analysis of this three-person competition (Figure 3.3).
Removing the Nevada caucus (which was heavily influenced by the high
number of Mormons who voted for their co-religionist, Romney), we can
see from the Table (3.3) that Romney and McCain were essentially tied
among somewhat conservative voters in New Hampshire and Florida.
Huckabee ran well among somewhat conservatives in the evangelical-
influenced states of Iowa and South Carolina, but Romney's support in
South Carolina was quite low while McCain's remained at the level he
had obtained elsewhere. After Thompson and Giuliani had left the race
following Florida, the race turned to the decisive middle stages.

DOI: 10.1057/9781137577535.0008

TABLE 3.3   *Candidate performance among somewhat conservative voters, 2008*

Primary/caucus	Date	Huckabee	McCain	Romney
Iowa (caucus)	January 3	34	18	27
New Hampshire	January 8	8	38	35
Michigan	January 15	17	32	35
South Carolina	January 19	30	32	17
Nevada (caucus)	January 19	5	13	56
Florida	January 29	14	35	32
Alabama	February 5	39	39	19
Arizona	February 5	6	54	35
Arkansas	February 5	55	26	13
California	February 5	12	45	34
Connecticut	February 5	5	51	37
Delaware	February 5	23	39	31
Georgia	February 5	33	31	34
Illinois	February 5	12	48	31
Massachusetts	February 5	2	28	65
Missouri	February 5	28	31	34
New Jersey	February 5	5	59	34
New York	February 5	11	53	32
Oklahoma	February 5	33	46	16
Tennessee	February 5	37	34	21
Utah	February 5	2	4	92
Louisiana	February 9	45	42	8*
Maryland	February 12	31	51	7*
Virginia	February 12	37	50	4*
Wisconsin	February 19	38	55	1*
Ohio	March 4	30	59	*
Texas	March 4	36	56	*
Vermont	March 4	11	76	*

*withdrew from race
Source: Weighted exit poll data, 2008.

In these races, it is notable that McCain's somewhat conservative support increased dramatically in states with a strong moderate (and a low evangelical) presence but never dropped below 30 percent in states that were not the homes of his competitors (see Table 3.3). Romney and Huckabee, however, varied widely in their support, Huckabee doing quite well in states with evangelical presences and Romney doing well in states with large metro areas but very poorly in largely rural, evangelical states.

What is perhaps most notable about these states is how closely Romney and Huckabee hewed to their pre-middle stage showings in states of each type. Huckabee received 34 and 30 percent of the somewhat conservative vote in the evangelical-influenced early states

DOI: 10.1057/9781137577535.0008

of Iowa and South Carolina. He received between 28 and 39 percent in each of the evangelical-influenced middle stage races, with his low mark coming in the less evangelical state of Missouri and his high coming in the Deep Southern, Baptist redoubt of Alabama. Huckabee's somewhat conservative strength outside these areas was incredibly low, showing how his support in the Southern states was more due to his religion than his fitting the typical somewhat conservative profile.

Romney's support exhibited nearly identical trends. He received 35 and 32 percent in the more moderate early states of New Hampshire and Florida. In the mid-stage moderate states, his support ranged from a low of 31 percent (Illinois) to a high of 38 percent (Connecticut). The departure of Giuliani and Thompson had no discernible effect on Romney's share of the vote in this key constituency. The same was true for him in evangelical states. Romney got only 17 percent in South Carolina: his showing in Alabama, Tennessee, and Oklahoma ranged between 16 and 21 percent. He did noticeably better in the urban areas of Missouri and Georgia, but even here his statewide total among somewhat conservatives reached only 34 percent.

Flanked on his religious right by Huckabee and his left by McCain, Romney could not win large enough shares of the somewhat conservative vote to win any of the major primaries on February 5, when 20 Republican contests were held. Within two days he was out, and the race was on to its final stage with only Huckabee and McCain remaining as competitive candidates.

This final stage of the nomination contest was marked by the obvious preference for McCain among most Romney voters. Table 3.3 shows that except in very religious Louisiana, Huckabee's share of the somewhat conservative vote remained mired in the 30–37 percent range he had received in the mid-stage primaries. McCain's share, however, shot upward. Even though each of the remaining states except Maryland had significant evangelical communities, McCain's range varied from a low of 42 percent (Louisiana) to a high of 59 percent (Ohio). He received a majority of the somewhat conservative vote in evangelical-tinged Virginia, reversing his performance there from eight years prior. And he received a whopping 56 percent of the somewhat conservative vote in Texas. Clearly the somewhat conservative voter who liked Romney in the mid-stages overwhelmingly chose the less conservative, but comparatively more statesmanlike, McCain.

DOI: 10.1057/9781137577535.0008

The 2012 nomination contest: Romney's firewall

The 2012 race was more like the 2000 race than 2008 for somewhat conservatives because one candidate—Bush in 2000, Romney in 2012— dispatched all of their potential rivals for the somewhat conservative vote early in the race. After the Tea Party exploded across the country in 2009–10, most Republican contenders were running far to the right to become the choice of the party's energetic, seemingly ascendant wing. Despite this, as many as five candidates could plausibly have laid claim to the somewhat conservative mantle in 2011. However, like Bush before him, Romney quickly maneuvered his potential competitors into either dropping out of the race entirely or discrediting themselves in the eyes of somewhat conservative voters.

Romney's first victim was former Minnesota Governor Tim Pawlenty. Pawlenty had won two terms in historically Democratic Minnesota, giving him a better electoral track record than his Massachusetts rival. He also was a fresh national face, without the stigma of Romney's losing 2008 run. However, he never distinguished himself successfully from Romney on issues. His laid back style also failed to energize donors or voters. National polls in the first half of 2011 showed Pawlenty far behind Romney, but also showed that his voter profile mimicked that of the man from Massachusetts: both men's voters shared similar characteristics in terms of income, education, and ideology (Gallup, Feb. 18-20, March 18-22, April 15-20, 2007). Thus, Pawlenty had to bring down Romney among somewhat conservatives since he was not attracting moderates or very conservative voters to his cause.

Despite this obvious challenge, Pawlenty failed to confront Romney effectively or forcefully. In June, he attacked "Obamneycare," noting the many similarities between Romney's Massachusetts health care reform and the Obama law that most Republicans hated. Just a few days later, however, Pawlenty walked back his criticism in a New Hampshire GOP debate despite being directly asked about his attack on Romney by the moderator. He never recovered. Two months after the debate, Pawlenty finished a weak third in the Iowa straw poll, behind Minnesota Congresswoman Michele Bachmann and Ron Paul. Out of funds, Pawlenty left the race.

Romney then faced potential competition for the party's establishment from former Utah Governor Jon Huntsman. Huntsman could have positioned himself as a more reliably Republican alternative to Romney,

DOI: 10.1057/9781137577535.0008

using as fodder Romney's many public changes of position on high-profile issues such as abortion. Huntsman, however, instead became better known for his belief in climate change and support for civil unions for same-sex couples, issues of little interest to even moderate Republican primary voters. He was also never able to explain satisfactorily why he accepted President Obama's appointment to become Ambassador to China, thereby alienating even somewhat conservatives, who strongly disliked the President. Despite being virtually a walking model for the establishment Republican, Huntsman allowed himself to be painted as a man of the center-left, not the center-right, which meant he never gained traction among the voters whose support he needed.

Romney then faced what would prove to be his strongest potential competitor, Texas Governor Rick Perry. Perry's potential was considerable. He was a strong evangelical and had great appeal to the very conservative religious voter. He was an early supporter of the Tea Party, sounding the anti-Washington populist themes they craved. His tax plan was straight out of the supply-side playbook, allowing him to appeal to the very conservative fiscal voter. And crucially, his ten years as a successful governor of America's largest Republican state meant he could demonstrate the maturity and gravitas somewhat conservative voters gravitate towards.

National polls released just after Perry's entrance into the race confirmed his cross-factional appeal. He led Romney by large margins among self-described very conservative voters, and was competitive with him among somewhat conservatives (Gallup, Aug. 17-21, 2007). Unlike the other potential challengers, Perry could conceivably win enough support to push Romney into electoral reliance on moderates alone, a fatal position for any Republican aspirant.

Perry's abysmal debate performances, however, quickly dissipated his support. He came across as out of his depth, slow witted, and unprepared to lead. While he retained some support among the more ideological factions, somewhat conservative voters saw a man who apparently had none of the personal characteristics they seek. By November Perry had plummeted in the polls, and he was never able to regain voters' trust.

Romney's final potential competitor, Newt Gingrich, then rose for his day in the sun. Like Perry, he was a Southerner with strong support from evangelical elements. Like Perry, very conservative voters with secular leanings thought he was potentially more steadfastly conservative than Romney. And like Perry, Gingrich had the stature and governing

DOI: 10.1057/9781137577535.0008

experience somewhat conservatives like. His twenty years in the House and four years as Speaker were not uncontroversial, but they did show Gingrich potentially had the ability not just to speak but to govern.

Gingrich put all of these virtues on display in the fall debates. Where Perry seemed confused, Newt exuded knowledge. Where Perry seemed awkward, Gingrich seemed assured. It should have been no surprise, then, that Gingrich rocketed up the national polls with a similar profile to Perry's as the Texas man fell (Gallup, Nov. 13-17, 2007).

Gingrich, however, was known for his volatility, his indiscipline, and his eagerness to embrace wild, out-of-the-box ideas. He had not been as steadfastly anti-government in the House as many fiscal conservatives desired. His tenure as Speaker was also rocked by some scandal, including his affair with a staffer whom he eventually divorced his second wife to marry. Thus, Gingrich was very vulnerable to counterattack among each of the three factions to whom he appealed, especially the somewhat conservatives who desire maturity above all else. Meanwhile, Romney was viewed favorably by a wide variety of Republican voters, cutting across ideological divisions (Sides and Vavreck 2013).

Romney used his vast fundraising advantage to good effect in December, filling the Iowa airwaves with attack ads against Gingrich. Predictably, the Gingrich wave started to crest, then fall, as the Iowa caucuses rolled into view. Iowa was not fertile ground for Romney because of the heavy influence wielded there by the faction most opposed to his candidacy, the very conservative evangelical. But having disposed of all challengers for the somewhat conservative vote, Romney had ensured he would not be wiped out in the Hawkeye State. Indeed, Romney finished a close second in the caucuses to former Pennsylvania Senator Rick Santorum.

Romney never relinquished his hold on the party's key voting bloc as the actual races unfolded (Figure 3.4). As Table 3.4 shows, he won majorities or near majorities among somewhat conservatives in every state without a dominant evangelical presence. Moreover, he retained about 30 percent of the somewhat conservative vote even in the Southern evangelical-influenced states whose races he would end up losing to either Santorum or Gingrich, such as Alabama, Georgia, Mississippi, Oklahoma, and Tennessee. None of his remaining competitors had sufficient appeal among this group to permit them to mount a serious challenge.

DOI: 10.1057/9781137577535.0008

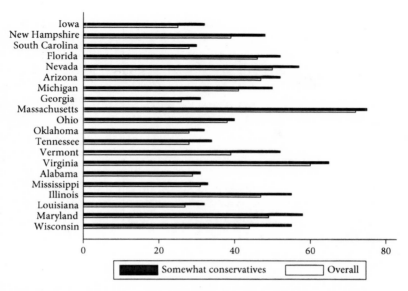

FIGURE 3.4   *Romney's relative performance among somewhat conservative voters, 2012*

Source: Weighted exit poll data, 2012.

TABLE 3.4   *Candidate performance among somewhat conservative voters, 2012*

Primary/caucus	Date	Gingrich	Paul	Romney	Santorum
Iowa (caucus)	January 3	16	21	32	19
New Hampshire	January 10	11	19	48	7
South Carolina	January 21	41	13	30	15
Florida	January 31	32	5	52	9
Nevada (caucus)	February 4	19	17	57	6
Arizona	February 28	15	8	52	25
Michigan	February 28	7	9	50	32
Georgia	March 6	47	5	31	16
Massachusetts	March 6	5	6	75	12
Ohio	March 6	16	9	40	34
Oklahoma	March 6	21	12	32	35
Tennessee	March 6	22	8	34	33
Vermont	March 6	10	15	52	22
Virginia	March 6	*	35	65	*
Alabama	March 13	33	3	31	31
Mississippi	March 13	31	4	33	31
Illinois	March 20	8	5	55	31
Louisiana	March 24	14	6	32	47
Maryland	April 3	9	8	58	25
Wisconsin	April 3	5	5	55	35

*Did not qualify for the ballot.
Source: Weighted exit poll data, 2012.

DOI: 10.1057/9781137577535.0008

We can see this most clearly by examining the way somewhat conservative voters moved as the race unfolded. First, note the relationship between Ron Paul's and Romney's support. Paul and Romney had been very polite to one another during the debates, much to the consternation of anti-Romney activists. This strategy seems to have paid off for Romney, as his share of somewhat conservative votes rose as Paul's fell. It appears that once the early races had established that Paul was not going to be the nominee, some of Paul's somewhat conservative voters moved to Romney as he was the man they found most congenial among the remaining serious candidates.

Second, note how both Gingrich and Santorum seem to have a hard ceiling on their level of somewhat conservative support. With the exception of Gingrich's home state of Georgia, neither man ever received more than 41 percent of the somewhat conservative vote. (Gingrich obtained this vote share in South Carolina, an evangelical-influenced state bordering his home.) Outside these two states, neither challenger received more than 35 percent of the somewhat conservative vote in any contested race.

Finally, note how Romney's vote share rose after Gingrich's losses to Santorum in Alabama and Mississippi effectively ended his campaign. Santorum's strategists had assumed that all of Gingrich's votes were anti-Romney and thus would flow to Santorum when Gingrich dropped out. Instead, Santorum's share of the somewhat conservative vote remained stuck in the low-to-mid-30s range that he had received during Gingrich's candidacy. Romney, however, moved up to 55 percent in both Illinois and Wisconsin, the highest shares he had received anywhere apart from the Mormon-influenced Nevada caucus. The implication is clear: somewhat conservative voters who preferred Gingrich found Romney more congenial than Santorum. Given these voters' demonstrated preference for stability and conservative consensus over change and confrontation, the ultimate result is not at all surprising. In addition to enjoying significant monetary advantages in the homestretch, Romney also had the backing of the Republican Party faction that matters most.

DOI: 10.1057/9781137577535.0008

Conclusion

No candidate becomes the nominee of the Republican Party without the support of at least a plurality of somewhat conservative voters, who lie at the median of the presidential primary electorate. Their support early on always establishes their favorite as one of the final competitors, and their support in later races always provides the ultimate winner with his margin of victory. The media may view somewhat conservative voters as difficult to find and less fun to cover, but they are the GOP's silent majority.

DOI: 10.1057/9781137577535.0008

4
Very Conservative Evangelicals

Abstract: *This group is small compared to the others, comprising around one-fifth of all GOP voters. They gain significant strength, however, from three unique factors. First, they are geographically concentrated in Southern and border states, where they can comprise a quarter or more of a state's electorate. Moreover, somewhat conservative voters in Southern and border states are also likelier to be evangelical, and they tend to vote for more socially conservative candidates than do their non-Southern, non-evangelical ideological cousins. Finally, they are very motivated to turn out in caucus states, such as Iowa and Kansas, and form the single largest bloc of voters in those races. These factors have given very conservative, evangelical-backed candidates unusual strength in Republican presidential contests.*

Keywords: evangelicals; presidential primaries; religion and politics; Republican Party

Olsen, Henry, and Dante J. Scala. *The Four Faces of the Republican Party: The Fight for the 2016 Presidential Nomination.* New York: Palgrave Macmillan, 2016. DOI: 10.1057/9781137577535.0009.

DOI: 10.1057/9781137577535.0009

The third-largest group is the moderates' bête noire: the very conserva-tive evangelicals.[1] This group is small compared to the others, compris-ing around one-fifth of all GOP voters. They gain significant strength, however, from three unique factors. First, they are geographically concentrated in Southern and border states, where they can comprise a quarter or more of a state's electorate. Moreover, somewhat conservative voters in Southern and border states are also likelier to be evangelical, and they tend to vote for more socially conservative candidates than do their non-Southern, non-evangelical ideological cousins. Finally, they are very motivated to turn out in caucus states, such as Iowa and Kansas, and form the single largest bloc of voters in those races.

These factors have given very conservative, evangelical-backed candidates unusual strength in Republican presidential contests. The evangelical favorite, for example, surprised pundits in two consecutive cycles: Mike Huckabee defeated a much better financed Mitt Romney in the 2008 Iowa caucuses, and Rick Santorum emerged from the bottom tier to triumph in Iowa four years later. Evangelicals also supplied the backing for evangelical leader Pat Robertson, who finished second in Iowa in 1988; and Pat Buchanan, who likewise finished second in the 1996 caucuses. Their strength in the Deep South and the border states also allowed Mike Huckabee rather than Mitt Romney to emerge as John McCain's final challenger in 2008. That strength, combined with their domination of the February 7 caucuses in Minnesota and Colorado, allowed Rick Santorum to emerge as Romney's challenger in 2012.

This group prefers candidates who are very open about their religious beliefs, place a high priority on social issues such as gay marriage and abortion, and see the United States in decline because of its movement away from the faith and moral codes of its traditionalist past. These voters view faith and belief, not reason and science, as the way to truth—a stance that puts them at odds with some members of their own party (Marietta and Barker 2007). Their concern with social issues such as abortion dates back to the days of Robertson and the Christian Right in the 1980s (Green and Guth 1988; Johnson et al. 1989; Langenbach and Green 1992; Oldfield 1996; Pastor et al. 1999; Wilcox 1992).

Their favored candidates tend to be economically more open to government intervention. Buchanan, for instance, opposed the North American Free Trade Agreement (NAFTA) in the 1990s.[2] Two decades later, Santorum wanted to create public policy that would reinvigorate manufacturing and bring back jobs to the American heartland. So far

DOI: 10.1057/9781137577535.0009

in 2016, Huckabee has come out against cuts in Social Security and Medicare (unlike many, more establishment-backed candidates), and Santorum has cast himself as the champion of blue-collar conservatives.

This social conservatism and economic moderation tends to place these candidates out of line with the center of the Republican Party, the somewhat conservative voter outside the Deep South. Each evangelical-backed candidate has lost this group decisively in primaries in the Midwest, Northeast, Pacific Coast, and mountain states. Indeed, they even lose them in Southern-tinged states like Virginia and Texas, where McCain's ability to win over somewhat conservative voters, coupled with huge margins among moderates and liberals, allowed him to hold off Huckabee in one-on-one face-offs during the 2008 nomination season.

Demographic profile

Very conservative evangelicals display a distinctive demographic profile within the Republican presidential primary electorate. Compared to other 2012 Republican primary voters (as reflected in numerous exit polls), they were less likely to possess a college education. They also were less likely to belong to a higher income bracket and more likely to live in small-town America. Of the four factions we examine here, they were by far the most likely to hail from the South: more than half said they lived there, compared to four of ten other Republican voters. Very conservative evangelicals were least likely to live in the East.

Party identification

Very conservative evangelicals identify overwhelmingly with the Republican Party (Table 4.1). In 2000, eight of ten described themselves as Republicans. This percentage increased in later cycles. In 2012, six out of seven described themselves as Republicans, compared to two-thirds of other Republican voters who participated in primaries and caucuses.

Very conservative evangelicals, however, were also highly supportive of the Tea Party movement that desired to rebel against the GOP party elite. In 2012, six of seven said they supported the movement, compared to half of other Republican voters.

DOI: 10.1057/9781137577535.0009

TABLE 4.1 *Profile of very conservative evangelical voters*

		Very conservative evangelicals	Other Republican primary voters
PARTY IDENTIFICATION			
Identify as Republican?	2008	88	72
	2012	84	64
TEA PARTY			
Support Tea Party	2012	85	53
ABORTION			
Should abortion be illegal in most or all cases?	2008	93	57
	2012	88	51
ISSUES			
Which issue mattered most in 2008?	Economy	27	42
	Illegal immigration	27	21
	Terrorism	25	15
	Iraq war	16	19
Which issues mattered most in 2012?			
	Economy	42	59
	Deficit	30	26
	Abortion	19	.7
CANDIDATE QUALITIES			
Which mattered most?			
2008	Shares my values	64	41
	Says what he believes	17	25
	Right experience	12	25
2012			
	Can defeat Obama	37	40
	True conservative	28	13
	Strong moral character	22	20
	Right experience	11	23

Source: Pooled and weighted exit poll data, 2008 and 2012. N. B.: Total number of respondents in 2008: 25,973; in 2012: 38,010. The number of respondents for each question, however, did vary.

DOI: 10.1057/9781137577535.0009

The presence of evangelicals in Republican primaries

During the 2000 Republican primaries, exit pollsters asked, "Do you consider yourself part of the conservative Christian political movement, also known as the religious right?" The likelihood that Republican voters would answer affirmatively depended heavily on the region from which they hailed. In portions of the Deep South, "religious right" voters represented 40 percent or more of the primary electorate. Of the nine states with 30 percent or more "religious right" voters, only one (Iowa) was outside the South. These voters comprised a quarter of primary voters in Ohio and Missouri, but just a tenth in Michigan. In Northeastern states and in California, fewer than one in five voters described themselves as such.

Twelve years later, little has changed about the power of evangelicals in Republican presidential primaries (Figure 4.1). Of those evangelicals who voted in the 2012 Republican presidential primaries, roughly four of ten described themselves as very conservative. This percentage

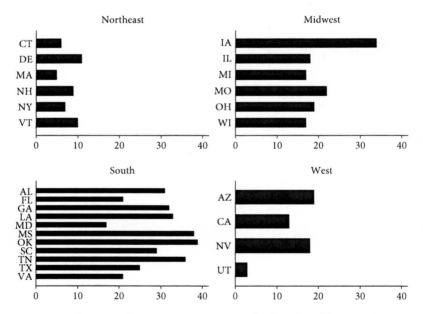

FIGURE 4.1   *Presence of very conservative evangelicals in Republican primaries and caucuses*

Source: Weighted exit poll data, 2008 and 2012.

DOI: 10.1057/9781137577535.0009

rose slightly in the South and the Midwest, and dipped slightly in the Northeast. (In the caucus states of the West, the proportion reached one-half.) During the 2012 primaries, very conservative evangelicals were a formidable force in Southern primaries, but much less so elsewhere in the country. In almost every Southern primary, more than 40 percent of voters identified themselves as both Tea Party and born-again. (The sole exceptions were Virginia and Florida, in which a third of voters did so.) In Alabama, Mississippi, Oklahoma, and Georgia, more than half of voters identified themselves as such.

Outside the South, the influence of these Tea Party evangelicals dropped sharply. They typically comprised between 25 and 30 percent of the primary electorate in Midwestern states. In the West, one out of three voters in Arizona was Tea Party evangelical. And in New England, the percentage dropped to less than one of six voters.

A similar pattern emerged among born-agains who described themselves as very conservative. These voters had the strongest presence in the Deep South states, such as Mississippi, Oklahoma, Tennessee, and Louisiana. They also were prominent in the Iowa caucuses. In the Midwest, and southern states such as Florida and Virginia, very conservative evangelicals were less than a quarter of the electorate. Finally, these voters were least prominent in New England.

Religiosity

Very conservative evangelicals are devoted practitioners of their religion. In 2008, four of five reported attending religious services at least weekly. Very conservative evangelicals' religiosity leads them to seek leaders who share their devotion. In 2008 and in 2012, nearly 90 percent said it mattered "a great deal or somewhat" that a candidate share their religious beliefs; in 2012, only six of ten other Republican voters agreed.

Preferences and priorities

Primary voters and candidates tend to hold similar positions on a variety of issues. On the issue of abortion, however, very conservative evangelicals take a distinctive stance. In 2000, almost half of self-described "Religious Right" voters participating in Republican presidential primaries said that abortion should be outlawed entirely, and more than eight out of ten "Religious Right" voters said it should be banned in most (if not all) cases. A decade later, very conservative evangelicals remained

DOI: 10.1057/9781137577535.0009

almost unanimous in their opposition to abortion, according to exit polls from 2008 and 2012. In contrast, other Republicans were divided on how much to restrict abortion, if at all. In 2012, almost half of very conservative evangelicals said that abortion should be outlawed in all circumstances, and almost 90 percent of very conservative evangelicals said abortion should be banned in most (if not all) cases.

Very conservative evangelicals also are much more likely to make abortion a high priority in their voting decisions, compared to their Republican peers. In 2000, one of six said that abortion was the issue that most influenced their voting decisions. In 2008, exit pollsters did not offer abortion to respondents as one of the most important issues. In 2012, one of five said abortion mattered most in deciding how they voted; just 7 percent of other Republican voters agreed.

In 2000 (and only then), exit pollsters offered "moral values" as one of the issues that mattered most in voting decisions. Half of very conservative evangelicals embraced this as their key issue. In 2008, exit pollsters did not include any social or moral issues among those possibly "most important" issues to voters, instead listing the economy, the war in Iraq, terrorism, and illegal immigration. Very conservative evangelicals were more likely to list terrorism as their most important issue than non-born agains, and less likely to state the economy (though the economy was most important for pluralities of both groups of voters).

Candidate qualities

More than any other faction of the Republican Party, very conservative evangelicals state that the most important quality for a candidate is that he stands up for conservative values.

In 2000, given seven different choices (including electability and leadership ability), four of ten very conservative evangelicals stated that representing conservative values was the candidate quality that most influenced their voting decisions.

In 2008, given four options, nearly two-thirds of very conservative evangelicals said that a candidate who "shares my values" was the quality most important to their vote choice. Other qualities, such as a candidate's electability, experience, or willingness to say what he believed, were far less critical to this bloc of voters. In comparison, slightly more than one-third of less conservative Republican primary voters agreed that a candidate who shared their values was most important.

DOI: 10.1057/9781137577535.0009

In 2012, a plurality of very conservative evangelicals agreed with a plurality of less conservative voters in the Republican Party that the ability to defeat Barack Obama was the candidate quality that mattered most. Very conservative evangelicals, however, were much more likely than other Republican voters to say that being a "true conservative" was their most important quality in a candidate—a greater percentage offered this answer, in fact, than said that "strong moral character" was most important. Very few cited right experience as their most important quality.

Given these facts, it is no surprise that George W. Bush and Huckabee have been the best examples of the sort of candidate very conservative evangelicals like. Bush was open about his faith in the early stages of the campaign and, unlike his father, openly courted leading evangelical pastors and activists. He was open about how his life had changed upon his conversion from a simple Protestant into an evangelical who possessed a personal relationship with Jesus Christ. He focused more on values and less on details than other candidates, and gave speeches (written by fellow evangelical Michael Gerson) that sounded themes and used language that resonated with evangelical audiences. The national media laughed, but Bush's 1999 statement that Jesus was his favorite political philosopher was music to these voters' ears.

Bush's rise in 1999 was due to many factors, but his ability to show very conservative evangelicals that he was plausibly one of them forestalled the emergence of a strong challenger to his right in the crucial Iowa caucuses. Despite this, he was not the overwhelming favorite of these voters early on. Two candidates, Gary Bauer and Alan Keyes, ran on much more fervent religious grounds, emphasizing abortion, social issues, and moral decline much more than Bush. Together, they received about 45 percent of the very conservative evangelical vote in Iowa, enough to keep Bush from obtaining a landslide victory.

Bush started to receive supermajority margins among these voters only after Bauer dropped out and the very moderate McCain emerged as Bush's primary challenger. As our theory would predict, once a voter's favorite drops out he or she makes a choice based on which of the remaining candidates looks most like their preferred choice. For the evangelical voter in 2000, that person was clearly their co-religionist Bush.

Huckabee in 2008 combined Bush's "one of us" status with Bauer and Keyes's greater emphasis on moral decline and social issues. He thus was able to win larger margins among these voters than Bush did in 2000.

DOI: 10.1057/9781137577535.0009

He was also able to retain their loyalty in the face of his narrow defeat in South Carolina and his failures in Michigan and Florida. An ordained Southern Baptist preacher, Huckabee was able to talk the talk in a way that Bush was unable (or unwilling) to do in 2000. These voters stuck with him despite many consecutive defeats in large part because neither of the candidates with supposed momentum, McCain and Romney, touched these voters' hearts and heads in the same way as Huckabee. Once Romney dropped out, the same dynamic that worked in Bush's favor in 2000 helped Huckabee gain even larger margins among very conservative evangelicals, who preferred one of their own to the relatively secular and moderate McCain.

How did evangelicals vote?

The 2000 nomination contest: Bush's favorite philosopher

Evangelicals had no shortage of suitors in 2000. Steve Forbes, who had run in 1996 as the very conservative secular candidate, trained his attention on building bridges with very conservative evangelicals. Bauer, a veteran of the Reagan administration who led the evangelical conservative think tank Family Research Council, joined the race. Keyes, another socially conservative veteran of the Reagan administration, was making his second consecutive run for the Republican nomination, with little hope of being more viable this time. Last but not least, Bush credited the late evangelist Billy Graham with planting the "mustard seed" in his soul that led him to "recommit my heart to Jesus Christ." (In 2004, Richard Land of the Southern Baptist Convention said of Bush, "This president expresses his faith in overtly evangelical terms in a way that is much more recognizable, much more identifiable as being quote, 'one of us' than the presidents that I've known in my lifetime" [Denton 2005]).

All of this was crucial in the run-up to the Iowa caucuses. Iowa Republicans have a very large evangelical component, one that is of crucial import in the low-turnout caucus. (Their favorite candidates do less well in Iowa's state primaries where more moderate Republicans are likelier to vote.) In 2000, Iowa's very conservative evangelicals broke into three nearly equal parts: Bush, Keyes, and Forbes all carried between 25 and 29 percent. (Bauer finished fourth amongst this group

DOI: 10.1057/9781137577535.0009

with 16.5 percent.) While Bush did not ride their support to victory, very conservative evangelicals provided the base[3] from which he could use his establishment backing to provide his victory margin. Indeed, Bush's establishment backing obscured what was to become clear in 2008 and 2012: no candidate can win Iowa from the right without plurality support from very conservative evangelicals.

McCain, in contrast, was raised as an Episcopalian, attended a Baptist church, and described himself as a Christian, but was not inclined toward public displays of faith. While he favored keeping "one nation, under God," in the Pledge of Allegiance, and described America as a "Christian nation," he also supported the separation of church and state. On the question of abortion, McCain criticized *Roe v. Wade* and called for its repeal, but did not favor a litmus test on *Roe* for Supreme Court nominees. McCain voted for the Defense of Marriage Act in 1996 that defined marriage as a heterosexual union, but said that the states, not the federal government, should govern marriage (Daniel and Holladay 2008). Infamously, in the February run-up to the pivotal Virginia primary, McCain denounced nationally prominent (and Virginia resident) evangelists Pat Robertson and Jerry Falwell as "agents of intolerance" and "corrupting influences on religion and politics." While McCain was not always so oppositional toward evangelical leaders, he sent numerous messages that their priorities were not his priorities.

Thus, even in the midst of McCain's landslide New Hampshire victory, the more religious candidates dominated among the small number of very conservative evangelicals in the Granite State. Keyes and Bush separated from Forbes there, each carrying more than 30 percent of their vote. Although Forbes made one last, futile stand in Delaware, the nomination contest had become a two-man race between Bush and McCain, with Keyes lingering as a third wheel.

Given the choice between two viable candidates for the nomination (and a non-viable third who made a special appeal to social conservatives), very conservative evangelicals swung strongly behind Bush (Figure 4.2). In every contest after New Hampshire, Bush carried a majority of very conservative evangelicals. On "Mega Tuesday" March 7, Bush won more than 70 percent of very conservative evangelicals in every state except for Massachusetts, where he carried six of ten. McCain's decision not to make himself acceptable to this group, coupled with Bush's long-standing determination to court them, meant that McCain's massive

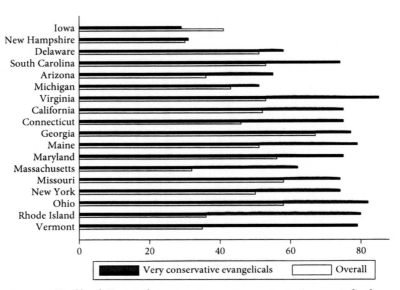

FIGURE 4.2   *Bush's relative performance among very conservative evangelicals, 2000*

Source: Weighted exit poll data, 2000.

TABLE 4.2   *Candidate performance among very conservative evangelicals, 2000*

Primary/caucus	Date	Bush	Forbes	Keyes	McCain
Iowa (caucus)	January 24	29	25	28	1
New Hampshire	February 1	31	10	38	12
Delaware	February 8	58	24	13	4
South Carolina	February 19	74	*	13	13
Arizona	February 22	55	*	9	35
Michigan	February 22	51	*	21	28
Virginia	February 29	85	*	8	6
California	March 7	75	*	11	12
Connecticut	March 7	75	*	9	17
Georgia	March 7	77	*	14	8
Maine	March 7	79	*	14	8
Maryland	March 7	75	*	21	4
Massachusetts	March 7	62	*	12	26
Missouri	March 7	74	*	13	8
New York	March 7	74	*	12	14
Ohio	March 7	82	*	9	9
Rhode Island	March 7	80	*	6	15
Vermont	March 7	79	*	4	17

* withdrew from race
Source: Weighted exit poll data, 2000.

DOI: 10.1057/9781137577535.0009

margin among moderates was usually more than outweighed by Bush's support from the religious right (Table 4.2).

A logistic regression of the Bush vote after the South Carolina primary until McCain ended his candidacy (Table 4.3) indicates that even after controlling for a host of demographic variables, the adherence of Southern conservative evangelicals to Bush was evident. As one might expect, Bush tended to perform better in his home region. But even after accounting for Bush's home-region advantage in the South, the more conservative a voter's ideology, the more likely that voter was to cast a vote for Bush. Finally, even after accounting for region and political ideology, a voter's identity as a member of the Religious Right remained a significant factor in support for Bush.

TABLE 4.3   *Logistic regression of Bush vote in 2000, post-South Carolina*

VARIABLES	Vote for Bush
Male	−0.20[***]
	(−4.83)
Age	0.05[*]
	(2.41)
Income	−0.00
	(−0.02)
Education	−0.13[***]
	(−6.61)
Religious Right	0.52[***]
	(9.86)
Republican	1.25[***]
	(28.21)
South	0.38[***]
	(7.85)
McCain Home State	−0.90[***]
	(−13.23)
Conservatism	0.51[***]
	(17.58)
Constant	−1.43[***]
	(−13.01)
N	16,058

t statistics in parentheses
[*] $p < 0.05$, [**] $p < 0.01$, [***] $p < 0.001$
Source: Pooled and weighted exit poll data, 2000.

DOI: 10.1057/9781137577535.0009

The 2008 nomination contest: 'One who comes from you'

One of Mitt Romney's chief obstacles to the Republican nomination was the distrust many evangelical Americans displayed toward his Mormon faith. In the run up to the Iowa caucuses, Romney offered a view of religion and politics similar to McCain's. In a speech reminiscent of John F. Kennedy's address to Protestant ministers in 1960, Romney asserted in 2007 that he did not "define my candidacy by my religion...no authorities of my church...will ever exert influence on presidential decisions." But Romney took pains to place religion at the center of his vision of America. He described Americans as "fundamentally a religious people," adding, "Freedom and religion endure together, or perish alone." Romney supported keeping God in the Pledge of Allegiance, as well as religious displays in public areas (Daniel and Holladay 2008).

Former Arkansas Governor and Baptist Minister Huckabee addressed his religiosity in a much less oblique fashion: "I come today as one not who comes to you, but as one who comes from you," he told the Values Voters Summit in the fall of 2007. He often told audiences that his faith was incorporated into his personal and professional life: "My faith is my life—it defines me." Huckabee supported constitutional amendments to outlaw abortion, and to define marriage as between one man and one woman, arguing "[Some of my opponents] do not want to change the Constitution, but I believe it's a lot easier to change the Constitution than it would be to change the word of the living God." But he was sometimes at odds with leaders of the religious right on questions of the government's role in the economy, immigration, and foreign policy. Many religious conservative elites, including Pat Robertson, elected to endorse other Republicans for president (DiSalvo and Copulsky 2009). He nevertheless parlayed this cultural similarity into becoming the very conservative evangelical's candidate of choice, especially among Southern Baptists, as national polling made clear even prior to the Iowa caucuses.

Iowa and New Hampshire: first-in-the-nation faction friction

Traditionally, the Iowa caucuses and the New Hampshire primary are viewed as generators of momentum and catalysts of consolidation. Jointly, these two contests have taken on the role of winnowing the field.

DOI: 10.1057/9781137577535.0009

In the 2008 Republican nomination process, Iowa and New Hampshire did again winnow the field, but rather than generating unstoppable momentum, they jointly created significant friction. New Hampshire put McCain, a champion of liberal and moderate Republicans, into the final round of competition for the nomination. And coming out of Iowa, another faction of the party, evangelicals (particularly southern evangelicals) had crowned a champion of their views and beliefs in Huckabee.

On the night of the Iowa caucuses, the former Arkansas governor had succeeded in pulling off an upset that had been weeks in the making. Evangelical voters apparently had considered Romney and rejected him, whether because of his Mormon religion, his history of social moderation, or both. Instead, they had chosen a candidate who appeared to be a more authentic representative of their views. The bond forged between Huckabee and evangelicals persisted throughout the remainder of the primaries.

The Huckabee faction

Conceivably, given Romney's support among mainstream and fiscal conservatives and many movement conservatives' antipathy toward McCain, Romney might have had a shot at the nomination despite his loss to McCain in New Hampshire by consolidating conservative support against the Arizona maverick. The allegiance of social conservatives and evangelicals to Huckabee, however, was always just enough to relegate Romney to "third-wheel" status in the three-way contest that developed after Florida. This was especially true in the Southern primaries, where McCain gained large numbers of delegates—not because of his prowess as a candidate, nor so much because of the momentum he gained as a frontrunner, but because of the GOP's winner-take-all rules or variants of that rule in two-thirds of the primaries, McCain was able to win a larger proportion of the delegates than he won in the popular vote. While Romney fared reasonably well among northern conservatives, Huckabee's appeal among southern conservatives, particularly evangelicals, gave McCain the breathing room he needed.

Huckabee won nearly half of very conservative evangelicals in Iowa, earning far more support than Romney (18 percent) or Fred Thompson (17 percent). In the contests to follow, Huckabee continued to perform well among very conservative evangelicals, although less strongly

DOI: 10.1057/9781137577535.0009

among weekly churchgoers in general (Kenski and Kenski 2010). Unsurprisingly, Huckabee performed best on his home soil, regularly carrying majorities or near-majorities in Southern states. But even far from home, Huckabee found a warm welcome among his fellow evangelicals. In the Midwest, he ran even with Romney among these voters in Romney's home state of Michigan (where his father had served as governor), and surpassed him in Illinois. Huckabee was even competitive with Romney among these voters (small in number though they were) in the Northeast, though he trailed him significantly in Western states such as Nevada and California (Table 4.4).

TABLE 4.4   *Candidate performance among very conservative evangelicals, 2008*

Primary/caucus	Date	Huckabee	McCain	Romney
Iowa (caucus)	January 3	46	5	18
New Hampshire	January 8	27	23	33
Michigan	January 15	35	11	35
South Carolina	January 19	48	19	12
Nevada (caucus)	January 19	24	6	38
Florida	January 29	33	19	37
Alabama	February 5	51	26	20
Arizona	February 5	24	26	41
Arkansas	February 5	72	8	16
California	February 5	29	21	42
Connecticut	February 5	41	12	44
Delaware	February 5	50	13	33
Georgia	February 5	49	16	32
Illinois	February 5	45	17	30
Massachusetts	February 5	20	18	57
Missouri	February 5	55	15	27
New Jersey	February 5	45	24	31
New York	February 5	37	26	33
Oklahoma	February 5	42	19	34
Tennessee	February 5	46	16	29
Utah	February 5	7	6	84
Louisiana	February 9	63	23	*
Maryland	February 12	60	24	*
Virginia	February 12	75	17	*
Wisconsin	February 19	72	20	*
Ohio	March 4	58	38	*
Texas	March 4	57	37	*
Vermont	March 4	57	31	*

* withdrew from race
Source: Weighted exit poll data, 2008.

DOI: 10.1057/9781137577535.0009

Romney's narrow losses on "Super Duper Tuesday" February 5 (on which 20 contests were held) demonstrate the problem he faced. Northeastern states had more secular conservatives, but were dominated by moderates. McCain easily won these states and Illinois on the strength of his moderate support, and by running slightly ahead of Romney among somewhat conservative, establishment Republican voters.

The Southern primary states featured many more very conservative voters and fewer moderates, but those so-called "movement conservative" voters were largely socially conservative evangelicals. Here Huckabee trounced Romney among the very conservative evangelicals whose support he desperately needed to counteract McCain's lead among the still sizeable moderates. Even though common wisdom had already narrowed the race down to two men, Romney and McCain, Huckabee's strength among voters who wanted religion and social issues placed front and center meant Romney had nowhere to go. Romney finished third in every Southern state, and Huckabee's losses to McCain in Missouri and Oklahoma meant McCain had built up a nearly insurmountable delegate lead over Romney, even before California's delegates were allocated.

Romney's campaign died in southern and central California. Even though the Golden State's conservatives tend to be secular and fiscally oriented in the classic Goldwater-Reagan mold, enough were Christian conservatives to allow McCain's huge margins among Bay Area moderates and small margins among somewhat conservatives to win nearly all of California's 170 delegates. Indeed, while Huckabee only won 12 percent statewide, he carried 26 percent among the one-third of voters who said they were evangelical Christians, only slightly less than Romney's 32 percent. Romney's failure to consolidate both very conservative factions – religious and secular -- under his leadership made clear what had been implied by Bush's 2000 campaign: no Republican candidate can win coming from the right without being the very conservative evangelical favorite.

After Romney dropped his bid for the nomination February 7, Huckabee consolidated the support of very conservative evangelicals (Figure 4.3). In every exit poll taken from February 9 to March 4, Huckabee carried a majority of these voters across a variety of Midwestern and Southern states, winning more than seven of ten of these voters in Wisconsin and Virginia. Huckabee succeeded in winning these voters despite widespread belief that McCain was very likely to be the Republican nominee.

DOI: 10.1057/9781137577535.0009

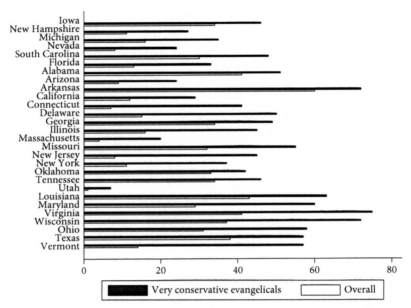

FIGURE 4.3   *Mike Huckabee's relative performance among very conservative evangelicals, 2008*

Source: Weighted exit poll data, 2008.

A logistic regression of the Huckabee vote after the South Carolina primary (Table 4.5, compiled from exit-poll data from various states) indicates that even after controlling for a host of demographic variables, the adherence of Southern conservative evangelicals to Huckabee is strikingly evident. As one might expect, Huckabee tended to perform better in his home region. But even after accounting for his home-region advantage, a voter's religious identity as born-again remained a powerful driver of allegiance to the Baptist pastor. Further, even after accounting for regional and religious identity, the more conservative a voter's ideology, the more likely that voter was to cast a vote for Huckabee. The fusion of social and religious identity and political ideology is one of the most powerful forces within the Republican Party today.

The 2012 nomination contest: Rise of Santorum

For most of the run-up to the Iowa caucuses, Rick Santorum was an afterthought. Despite a two-term U.S. Senate career that culminated in a leadership position, Santorum's nearly 20-point 2006 defeat to Democrat

DOI: 10.1057/9781137577535.0009

TABLE 4.5 *Logistic regression of Huckabee vote in 2008, post-South Carolina*

VARIABLES	Vote for Huckabee
Male	−0.18[**]
	(−3.08)
Age	−0.23[***]
	(−7.55)
Education	−0.06
	(−1.89)
Income	0.01
	(0.61)
Evangelical	1.50[***]
	(22.50)
Population Density	−0.22[***]
	(−4.94)
South	0.53[***]
	(7.77)
Republican	−0.18[*]
	(−2.43)
Conservatism	0.34[***]
	(8.85)
Huckabee Home State	1.28[***]
	(12.89)
Romney Home State	−1.04[***]
	(−5.21)
McCain Home State	−0.62[***]
	(−4.01)
Constant	−1.72[***]
	(−9.44)
N	11,501

t statistics in parentheses
[*] $p < 0.05$, [**] $p < 0.01$, [***] $p < 0.001$
Source: Pooled and weighted exit poll data, 2008.

Bob Casey in Pennsylvania, combined with his vocal social conservatism, meant virtually all observers wrote off his presidential nomination bid as little more than a vanity run. Languishing at the bottom of the polls and continually strapped for campaign cash, Santorum appeared to be the one conservative alternative to Romney who would never gain momentum. As late as December 2011 (December 7-11, Pew), Santorum was in

DOI: 10.1057/9781137577535.0009

low single-digits in national polls and among evangelical voters. Even among very conservative evangelicals, his ultimate core vote, Santorum had the support of fewer than one in 10 at a time when Newt Gingrich enjoyed backing from almost a third.

But Santorum began to rise just days before the Iowa caucuses, which had been his nearly sole focus throughout 2011. On the night of the caucuses, Santorum achieved a narrow victory over Romney (although it was not recognized until a recount was concluded several weeks later). Santorum achieved his victory with his relative dominance among very conservative evangelicals, carrying roughly four of ten such voters. Beyond Santorum, the very conservative evangelical vote splintered, with no candidate winning more than 20 percent. Romney had the support of just 10 percent.

Within two weeks after the Iowa caucuses (Pew, January 11-16), Gingrich's support among evangelicals had collapsed in national polls and Santorum's had tripled. Voters in states holding primaries, however, were even more dynamic (Figure 4.4). Very conservative evangelicals continued to reject Romney, even as he emerged as the frontrunner after

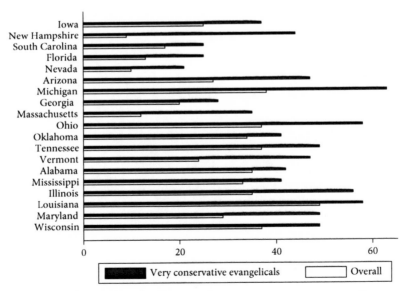

FIGURE 4.4   *Rick Santorum's relative performance among very conservative evangelicals, 2012*

Source: Weighted exit poll data, 2012.

DOI: 10.1057/9781137577535.0009

Iowa and New Hampshire. (In New Hampshire, a state in which Romney did well among virtually every segment of the Republican electorate, he finished fourth among very conservative evangelicals.) This was especially true in the South. In South Carolina, where Romney suffered a double-digit defeat to Gingrich statewide, he only won the support of one of seven very conservative evangelicals.

This set the tone for virtually every Southern state to follow: Romney routinely finished with no more than 20–25 percent of the conservative evangelical vote, even in late primaries when Romney's nomination was all but assured. (The conspicuous exception to this was Virginia, where Romney won a majority; in this state, neither Gingrich nor Santorum qualified for the ballot. The only other candidate on the ballot was Ron Paul.) Even in Midwestern states that Romney carried, such as Ohio, Wisconsin, and Illinois, he regularly finished far behind Santorum among conservative evangelicals.

After Santorum won three contests February 7 with very conservative evangelical support, his standing among very conservative evangelicals nationally skyrocketed—though at the same time, not without limitations (Pew, February 8-12). In a four-man race, about half now supported Santorum, more than five times the level of support for Romney. The support of very conservative evangelicals undergirded his plurality among all born-agains. Less conservative evangelicals were notably less enthusiastic about Santorum.

The presence of both Gingrich and Santorum as challengers to Romney in the early and intermediate stages of the nomination contest disrupted the unity of very conservative evangelicals observed in the 2000 and 2008 presidential primaries. Santorum, in particular, enjoyed a significant regional advantage in the Midwest, near his home state of Pennsylvania. He won outright majorities of very conservative evangelicals in Michigan, Ohio, and Illinois, and led with half of this vote in Wisconsin. In the South, very conservative evangelicals first rallied to Gingrich, but he lost that lead to Santorum in primaries held after Santorum's February 7 trifecta (Table 4.6).

A logistic regression of Republican presidential primary voters in 2012 after the carve-out states (Table 2.7) bears this out. It indicates the strength of the resistance of very conservative evangelicals to Romney's nomination. Even after accounting for a host of demographic variables, the more conservative the voter, the less likely that voter was to support Romney. If that voter also hailed from the South, support for

TABLE 4.6   *Candidate performance among very conservative evangelicals, 2012*

Primary/caucus	Date	Gingrich	Romney	Santorum
Iowa (caucus)	January 3	14	10	37
New Hampshire	January 10	22	15	44
South Carolina	January 21	50	14	25
Florida	January 31	43	25	25
Nevada (caucus)	February 4	33	32	21
Arizona	February 28	17	29	47
Michigan	February 28	6	25	63
Georgia	March 6	53	15	28
Massachusetts	March 6	7	44	35
Ohio	March 6	13	23	58
Oklahoma	March 6	30	23	41
Tennessee	March 6	26	17	49
Vermont	March 6	10	28	47
Virginia	March 6	*	60	*
Alabama	March 13	35	17	42
Mississippi	March 13	34	21	41
Illinois	March 20	8	33	56
Louisiana	March 24	17	19	58
Maryland	April 3	16	30	49
Wisconsin	April 3	5	36	49

* did not qualify for ballot
Source: Weighted exit poll data, 2012.

Romney became even less likely. And even after accounting for region and ideology, a voter's religious identity as a born-again remained a significant negative factor working against Romney. Both Gingrich and Santorum fared better among more conservative voters, according to a logistic regression of their respective vote support after the Florida primary (Tables 4.7 and 4.8). Gingrich, however, enjoyed a home-region advantage in the South that Santorum obviously lacked. Santorum's key strengths, in contrast, were tied both to voter ideology and voters' religious identity as born-agains.

Ultimately, the Gingrich and Santorum campaigns fatally wounded each other. In the early races (South Carolina and Florida), Santorum's presence in the race either held Gingrich's margin down (in South Carolina) or contributed mightily to his margin of defeat (in Florida). Both results underwrote the narrative that Gingrich could not defeat Romney, leading very conservative evangelicals in later states to consider Santorum. However, Gingrich's refusal to leave the race after Florida

DOI: 10.1057/9781137577535.0009

TABLE 4.7   *Logistic regression of Gingrich primary vote in 2012, post-Florida*

VARIABLES	Vote for Gingrich
Male	0.15"
	(3.16)
Age	0.23"'
	(8.51)
Education	−0.18"'
	(−6.68)
Income	−0.05'
	(−2.32)
Evangelical	0.16"
	(3.10)
Population Density	0.01
	(0.15)
South	0.79"'
	(14.86)
Republican	0.17"
	(2.75)
Conservatism	0.18"'
	(6.30)
Romney Home State	−0.78"'
	(−5.05)
Gingrich Home State	1.13"'
	(18.13)
Constant	−2.83"'
	(−18.93)
N	23,053

t statistics in parentheses
' $p < 0.05$, " $p < 0.01$, "' $p < 0.001$
Source: Pooled and weighted exit poll data, 2012.

meant that his presence on the ballot continued to draw some very conservative evangelical votes away from Santorum in the intermediate stages, especially in the South. This limited Santorum's ability to win in the Midwest (Gingrich's presence might have cost Santorum Ohio) and meant that Santorum's Southern victories were too narrow to give him the delegates he needed to be a plausible nominee.

Santorum's loss, however, ultimately arose from the same factor that killed Huckabee: he simply had little appeal among the other three factions. Santorum had his devotees, but moderates, somewhat

TABLE 4.8   *Logistic regression of Santorum primary vote in 2012, post-Florida*

VARIABLES	Vote for Santorum
Male	-0.15^{***}
	(-4.06)
Age	-0.15^{***}
	(-6.77)
Education	0.02
	(0.78)
Income	-0.05^{**}
	(-2.96)
Evangelical	0.67^{***}
	(15.97)
Population Density	0.11^{***}
	(3.92)
South	0.05
	(1.18)
Republican	-0.11^{*}
	(-2.53)
Conservatism	0.31^{***}
	(12.66)
Romney Home State	-0.93^{***}
	(-9.84)
Gingrich Home State	-0.82^{***}
	(-11.29)
Constant	-1.26^{***}
	(-9.13)
N	23,053

t statistics in parentheses
$^{*}p < 0.05$, $^{**}p < 0.01$, $^{***}p < 0.001$
Source: Pooled and weighted exit poll data.

conservatives, and very conservative secular voters all tended to prefer Romney over him when presented with a choice between the two.

These races show both the power and the limitations on the power of very conservative evangelicals. Their support is crucial to anyone trying to unite the right in a bid for the nomination. But such a candidate must be primarily defined in non-religious ways, as Bush was in 2000, if that candidate has any realistic chance of becoming the Republican nominee.

DOI: 10.1057/9781137577535.0009

Notes

1   Exit pollsters determine whether voters are evangelicals by simply asking
    them whether they identify themselves as such. Scholars identify evangelicals
    via three methods. First, they consider the denomination of their church:
    Some churches belong to the National Association of Evangelicals, while
    others do not. Another option is to consider whether they subscribe to a set
    of religious beliefs or doctrine. These beliefs would include accepting the
    divine Christ as the path to eternal salvation, as well as acceptance of the
    Bible as error-free truth. Third, evangelicals are often referred to as "born-
    agains" because of their personal experience of spiritual rebirth from the
    Holy Spirit (Wilcox 1992).
2   For a contrary view on Buchanan voters, see Weakliem (2001).
3   Iowa produces an interesting bit of trivia that can inform journalists and
    analysts wishing to understand how these voters think and where they will
    swing. Two counties in the far northwest of the state, Sioux and Lyon, were
    settled in the 19th century by very conservative members of the Dutch
    Reformed Church. These counties invariably support the most socially
    conservative, religiously oriented candidate in the Iowa caucus. They backed
    Pat Buchanan in 1996, Bauer in 2000, Huckabee in 2008, and Santorum in
    2012. Someone wishing to understand how these voters will swing in 2016
    can learn a lot by regularly visiting these counties.

DOI: 10.1057/9781137577535.0009

5

Very Conservative Seculars

Abstract: *Washington D.C. elites are most familiar with this faction, and as a result tend to overrate their power. In reality, this group comprises a small percentage of Republican primary voters nationwide, and thus never sees its choice emerge from the initial races to contend in later stages. Candidates who represent this faction also have difficulties forming coalitions. Secular moderates and somewhat conservative voters prefer candidates with less materialistic, sweeping economic radicalism while very conservative evangelicals flock to someone singing from their hymnal.*

Keywords: conservatism; ideology; presidential elections; presidential primaries; Republican Party

Olsen, Henry, and Dante J. Scala. *The Four Faces of the Republican Party: The Fight for the 2016 Presidential Nomination.* New York: Palgrave Macmillan, 2016. DOI: 10.1057/9781137577535.0010.

DOI: 10.1057/9781137577535.0010

The final and smallest Republican tribe is the one that Beltway elites in Washington, DC are most familiar with: very conservative, secular voters. This group comprises about 10 percent nationwide and thus never sees its choice emerge from the initial races to contend in later stages. Jack Kemp and Pete DuPont in 1988; Steve Forbes or Phil Gramm in 1996 (and Forbes again in 2000); Fred Thompson or Mitt Romney in 2008; Herman Cain, Rick Perry, or Newt Gingrich in 2012: each of these candidates showed promise in early polling but foundered in early contests once voters became more familiar with each of them. Secular moderates and somewhat conservative voters preferred candidates with less materialistic, sweeping economic radicalism while very conservative evangelicals went with someone singing from their hymnal. Thus, these voters quickly had to choose which of the remaining candidates to support in subsequent races after their favorite dropped out.

This small but influential bloc likes urbane, fiscally oriented men. For example, in 1988 they preferred Ronald Reagan's successor to be Kemp, the author of massive tax-cut legislation in Reagan's first term; or DuPont, an advocate for ending farm subsidies and privatizing Social Security. A quarter-century later, this group was tempted by Perry until his lack of sophistication became painfully obvious in the early debates. It then flirted with Gingrich until his temperamental issues resurfaced in Florida. After that, faced with the choice of Rick Santorum or Mitt Romney, it swung behind Romney en masse.

The latter example is in fact this group's modus operandi. They invariably see their preferred candidate knocked out early, and they then invariably gravitate toward whoever is backed by the somewhat conservative bloc. Forbes's early exit from the 2000 race, for example, was crucial to George W. Bush's ability to win South Carolina against John McCain's onslaught. In New Hampshire, Bush won only 34 percent of the very conservative vote; Forbes received 23 percent. With Forbes out of the race, however, Bush was able to capture 72 percent of the very conservative vote in South Carolina.

Demographic profile

Very conservative seculars display a distinctive demographic profile within the Republican presidential primary electorate. Compared to other primary voters in 2012, they were more likely to possess a college education. They also were more likely to belong to a higher income bracket. They were more likely to live in a large city, and less likely to live in small-town America. Of the four factions we have examined here, they were less likely to hail from the South and more likely to call the West their home. This picture of very conservative secular voters, compared to that of very conservative evangelicals, gives a sense of the gulf between these two factions of the Republican Party. While they share a common self-identification that they are more conservative than most of their fellow party members, their backgrounds are quite different. And while their ideological self-identification is identical, the content of their conservatism may well differ significantly.

The presence of very conservative seculars in Republican primaries

To estimate the presence of very conservative seculars in the 2012 Republican primaries, we examined the percentage of very conservative primary voters who did not describe themselves as born-again (Figure 5.1). The only contest in which very conservative seculars

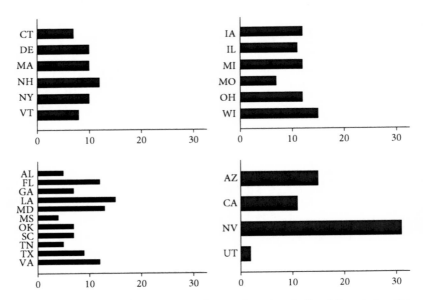

FIGURE 5.1   *Presence of very conservative secular voters in Republican primaries and caucuses*

Source: Weighted exit poll data, 2008 and 2012.

DOI: 10.1057/9781137577535.0010

exceeded 20 percent was the Nevada caucuses, where they comprised almost a third of the electorate. In most states (including the Iowa caucuses), this bloc of voters only comprised 10–15 percent of the primary electorate. The percentage fell below 10 percent in several states in the Deep South.

The 2000 exit polls generally lacked questions on religiosity, other than a query about whether voters considered themselves part of the Religious Right. Therefore, in order to estimate the percentage of very conservative seculars participating in the 2000 primaries, we examined very conservative voters who did not describe themselves as Religious Right.

The 2008 exit polls offered the most detail on voters' religiosity. In particular, voters were queried as to how often they attended religious services. Thus we measured very conservative seculars as those very conservative voters who did not attend services regularly, that is, once a week or more.

In 2012, exit pollsters asked the religious attendance question only sporadically. So we were forced to measure very conservative seculars as those very conservative voters who did not describe themselves as born-again or evangelical.

Where's the Tea Party?

In the 2012 exit polls, voters were asked about their adherence to the "Tea Party," a movement which sprang up in the aftermath of the federal bail-outs and massive stimulus of 2008 and 2009. Republican primary voters who expressed adherence or sympathy toward the Tea Party could be divided into two groups: "Born-again" or evangelical Tea Party support-ers, and those Tea Party adherents who said they were not evangelical Christians. We used the latter here as an (admittedly rough) measure of very conservative seculars.

At first glance, it is mildly surprising that three of the four states with the highest percentage of secular conservatives are in the Northeast (Maryland, Massachusetts, and New Hampshire). Remember, however, that the Northeast also had very low percentages of "born-again" Tea Party supporters (see Chapter 4). In each of these states, slightly more than a third were secular conservatives.

DOI: 10.1057/9781137577535.0010

TABLE 5.1   *Profile of very conservative secular voters*

		Very conservative seculars	Other Republican primary voters
PARTY IDENTIFICATION			
Identify as Republican?	2008	85	74
	2012	82	67
TEA PARTY			
Support Tea Party?	2012	83	58
ABORTION			
Should abortion be illegal in most or all cases?	2008	72	62
	2012	66	59
ISSUES			
Which issue mattered most in 2008?	Illegal immigration	35	22
	Economy	25	40
	Terrorism	22	16
	War in Iraq	16	19
Which issues mattered most in 2012?			
	Economy	51	56
	Federal budget deficit	34	26
	Abortion	7	10
CANDIDATE QUALITIES Which mattered most?			
2008	Shares my values	52	44
	Says what he believes	20	24
	Right experience	19	23
2012			
	Can defeat Obama	47	39
	True conservative	26	15
	Strong moral character	13	22
	Right experience	13	21

Source: Pooled and weighted exit poll data, 2008 and 2012. N. B.: Total number of respondents in 2008: 25,973; in 2012: 38,010. The number of respondents for each question, however, did vary.

In Midwestern primaries, very conservative seculars comprised 25–30 percent of the electorate. The only exception to this was the Iowa caucuses, which had a high percentage of born-again Tea Partiers, but only about 20 percent of the electorate classified as very conservative seculars.

DOI: 10.1057/9781137577535.0010

The greatest variation in the strength of very conservative seculars appeared in the Southern primaries. Again, an inverse relationship appears between the percentage of very conservative seculars and the percentage of born-again Tea Party adherents. In Southern states with high percentages of born-again Tea Partiers (such as Alabama, Mississippi, Oklahoma, and Tennessee), less than 20 percent of the electorate were classified as very conservative seculars. Florida and Virginia, which had low percentages of born-agains, had a higher proportion of very conservative secular Tea Party supporters.

These measures, however, certainly overstate the number of very conservative seculars because this method includes those somewhat conservative voters with strong Tea Party leanings. Thus, we should view this measure more as a quantification of "fiscal and constitutional first" conservatives, that is, conservatives who prioritize tax cuts and limited government over values or social issues, than the sort of very conservative secular who might have preferred, for example, Steve Forbes to Bush in the early portion of the 2000 nomination cycle.

In the West, Arizona followed the pattern in Virginia and Florida. The Nevada caucuses had an unusually high number of very conservative seculars, more than 50 percent. Nevada's figure might be unnaturally high, however, because of the large number of Mormons who participated in the 2012 caucus. Mormons are socially conservative, but their theology does not permit them to claim to be "born-again." However, as we note in chapter 6, Nevada and other Western states have a demonstrably higher share of "soft libertarians"[1] in their electorates. Mormons were approximately 25 percent of the 2012 GOP Nevada electorate, so even if all of them were Tea Party non-born agains, a highly unlikely occurrence, Nevada would still have a very high share of very conservative seculars.

Issue priorities

In the 2000 primaries, very conservative seculars closely resembled their somewhat conservative counterparts in terms of key issues that affected their vote choice. A plurality (about one-third) said that "moral values"—a catchphrase that apparently referred to misconduct during the Clinton administration, including the Monica Lewinsky affair—mattered most in determining their chosen candidate. Another quarter cited taxes as their key issue.

DOI: 10.1057/9781137577535.0010

In the 2008 cycle, however, very conservative seculars displayed a distinctive set of issue priorities. More than a third cited illegal immigration as the most important issue facing the country, a higher percentage than existed among less conservative voters. One of four cited the economy, a percentage that was lower than among less conservative voters. They were also more likely to mention terrorism as a key issue, though less likely to mention the war in Iraq.

During the 2012 primaries, while half of this voting bloc cited the economy as their key issue, this was a lower percentage than among their less conservative counterparts. As a bloc, these voters were more likely to choose the federal deficit as their most important issue.

Secularism and abortion

Only one of four very secular conservatives said in 2008 that it mattered a great deal that their candidate shared common religious beliefs with him – a percentage much closer to moderates and liberals than very conservative evangelicals. Very secular conservatives consistently are more likely to favor an outright ban on abortion, compared to their more moderate peers in the Republican primary electorate. Compared to very conservative evangelicals, however, they are quite unlikely to label abortion as an issue of utmost importance.

From 2000 to 2012, a large majority (between six and seven out of ten) favored serious restrictions on abortion. Between a fifth and a quarter said that abortion should be prohibited in all cases, a portion much larger than that found among less conservative Republican voters. However, only a small percentage (less than 10 percent) named abortion as the issue that mattered most for their voting decisions, especially compared to their very conservative religious brethren.

Candidate qualities

Very conservative secular voters consistently express preferences for a candidate who would champion conservative values. In 2000, when asked which candidate quality mattered most in their voting decisions, a plurality (more than a third) said a candidate who represented

DOI: 10.1057/9781137577535.0010

conservative values. Very conservative seculars were more likely to offer this answer than their less conservative peers.

In 2008, exit pollsters did not offer respondents "represent conservative values" as a possible response for most important quality in a candidate. Respondents were asked, however, whether finding a candidate who "shares my values" was the most important factor in their vote choice—and half of very conservative seculars cited it, a far higher percentage than less conservative voters. Very conservative seculars were also less likely than less conservative factions of the party to point to a candidate's experience as decisive in their vote choice.

In the 2012 primaries, very conservative seculars were more likely than less conservative primary voters to cite electability—specifically, finding a candidate who could defeat Barack Obama—as the most important factor in their vote choice. (Almost half said so.) Beyond electability, however, this bloc once again was more likely to cite ideology—specifically, whether the candidate was a true conservative—as key to their decision. And once again, they were less likely to choose experience as especially important.

In sum, very conservative seculars often identify themselves as "movement conservatives": people who believe that the American traditions and way of life enshrined in the Declaration of Independence and the Constitution are eroding quickly and that immediate action is needed to stem the tide and reverse course.

Finding a champion

The 2000 nomination contest: Satisfied with second-best

The establishment favorite, George W. Bush, appeared to face a considerable challenge to his right from millionaire publisher Steve Forbes. This was Forbes's second attempt to win the nomination of his party. In 1996, as a political neophyte, Forbes was derided in the media for his awkward campaign style, but he ultimately won two primaries (Arizona and Delaware) and collected more than 1.7 million votes overall, third behind Pat Buchanan and nominee Bob Dole. The threat of Forbes self-funding another presidential campaign in 2000 spurred the Bush campaign to forego matching public funding for the primaries, thus allowing it to ignore the cap on primary spending—a precedent that all subsequent

DOI: 10.1057/9781137577535.0010

nominees of both major parties would follow. Bush wound up raising more than $95 million (Hasen 2009).

Forbes was a potential threat to Bush because of his great appeal to the very conservative secular voter. In many ways, he was the archetype of what they wanted. A successful businessman who lived in Manhattan and owned a luxurious yacht, Forbes focused on how free minds and free markets could create wealth and enhance happiness. He was best known for his then-pioneering flat tax proposal, but his 1996 platform included many other market-based reforms that are now conservative staples, such as medical savings accounts and school vouchers. While not unreligious, Forbes clearly did not view American culture as being in decline and did not invoke his faith as the underpinning of his public life. Indeed, in 1996 he was attacked by religious conservatives for owning a photograph from the infamous Robert Mapplethorpe, whose publicly-funded sado-masochistic pictures had made him a cause celebre among social conservatives. (The picture Forbes owned was not pornographic at all, which demonstrates the wide gulf between his and the religious right's cultural sensibilities.) Forbes's appeal and worldview were on full display in the December 1999 debate, during which Bush famously said Jesus Christ was his favorite political philosopher. Forbes confidently said his favorite was John Locke, the English Enlightenment philosopher often considered the father of modern, limited government conservatism.

Recognizing the potential threat from Forbes, Bush promulgated his own tax cut plan in the fall of 1999. By embracing significant tax cuts for all, with a large reduction in the top marginal rate paid only by the wealthiest taxpayers, Bush showed very conservative seculars that he, too, shared their concerns. Bush would never touch the hearts of the supply-side faithful, but those less fervent in their secular fiscal faith could support him in good conscience.

In the run-up to the 2000 primaries, however, Forbes also faced competition on his right from an unlikely source. Alan Keyes, a former United Nations ambassador during the Reagan administration, also had decided to make a second run at his party's nomination, after experiencing little success in his first attempt in 1996. Keyes was a good example of a type of presidential campaign that has become a persistent part of the presidential nomination process: low-spending, long-duration campaigns, featuring candidates who raise little money but nonetheless remain in business with "low budget campaign tactics" (Norrander 2006). These candidates survive by filling an "electoral niche" within the field of candidates (Steger

DOI: 10.1057/9781137577535.0010

et al. 2002). They aim to appeal to a portion of the party. These candidates tend to be "policy seekers," those whose first priority is not necessarily to win the nomination, but rather to influence the party agenda and advocate for "particular policy outcomes." These candidates also tend to draw from one particular party faction, in terms of voters and contributors; as a result, they do not require the financial resources that candidates with a plausible chance of winning the office need to possess.

Keyes had appeal to both very conservative factions. He was fervently pro-life and invoked cultural decline in his stump talks, as we mentioned in Chapter 4. As a student of conservative political philosopher Harvey Mansfield, he also was well versed in American political thought, and easily invoked the themes of constitutionalism and strictly limited government that resonates among very conservative seculars. Forbes thus was not the only candidate with appeal to the Constitution-loving, small-government, low-tax crowd.

These challenges proved fatal to Forbes. In Iowa, Bush bested Forbes by double digits among very conservative seculars, winning more than 40 percent of the vote in this faction. Forbes won only three of ten very conservative seculars, while Keyes finished third, carrying one of six of these voters. Keyes also performed at the same level in New Hampshire, finishing roughly even with Forbes among these voters.

When Forbes left the race after losing Delaware, very conservative seculars united behind the one viable candidate amenable to them (Figure 5.2). In South Carolina, Bush outperformed McCain among these voters by a 3-1 margin. In every following contest but one, Bush carried a majority of these voters. This was in part because of Forbes's endorsement of Bush and in part because of Bush's own appeal, but it was also in part because McCain ostentatiously refused to cut taxes for the top bracket. This "no tax cuts for the rich" mantra helped him with moderates, but it hurt him among the former Forbes backers for whom belief in trickle-down, supply-side economics was an article of faith. Bush, being the more acceptable of the two candidates, was the grateful beneficiary of their belief (Table 5.2).

The 2008 nomination contest: Romney as conservative alternative?

Mitt Romney will be remembered in presidential campaign history as a moderate Republican from the Northeast who struggled and ultimately succeeded in becoming the nominee of an increasingly conservative

DOI: 10.1057/9781137577535.0010

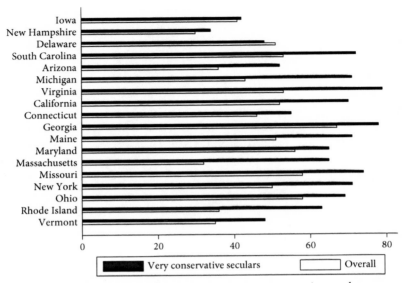

FIGURE 5.2   *Bush's relative performance among very conservative seculars, 2000*
Source: Weighted exit poll data, 2000.

TABLE 5.2   *Candidate performance among very conservative secular voters, 2000*

Primary/caucus	Date	Bush	Forbes	Keyes	McCain
Iowa (caucus)	January 24	42	31	19	2
New Hampshire	February 1	34	23	18	23
Delaware	February 8	48	27	9	15
South Carolina	February 19	72	*	6	22
Arizona	February 22	52	*	6	41
Michigan	February 22	71	*	11	17
Virginia	February 29	79	*	5	16
California	March 7	70	*	10	19
Connecticut	March 7	55	*	5	31
Georgia	March 7	78	*	6	16
Maine	March 7	71	*	5	22
Maryland	March 7	65	*	18	17
Massachusetts	March 7	65	*	6	28
Missouri	March 7	74	*	8	16
New York	March 7	71	*	12	17
Ohio	March 7	69	*	8	23
Rhode Island	March 7	63	*	5	32
Vermont	March 7	48	*	7	43

* Withdrew from race
Source: Weighted exit poll data, 2000.

DOI: 10.1057/9781137577535.0010

party. This narrative, however, overlooks the fact that Romney's 2008 strategy was to set himself up not as the reincarnation of his father, nor as a traditional Rockefeller Republican, but as the conservative alternative to McCain. Romney's failure to capture the nomination on his first attempt should not obscure his success in courting very conservative secular voters during the 2008 cycle.

While very conservative evangelicals found Romney lacking the authenticity they craved from Mike Huckabee, very conservative seculars found much to like: an urbane, well-educated conservative with a business background who would focus his presidency on the economy and national security. Romney signed conservative activist Grover Norquist's "no new tax" pledge and agreed to support a balanced budget amendment to the Constitution. He also reversed his earlier support for greenhouse gas emission restrictions and for legal abortion while moving toward more mainstream conservative positions on gun control and immigration. In a field without a Forbes-like candidate to excite very conservative seculars, Romney's gambit paid off. In a national poll the month prior to the Iowa caucuses (Pew, December 19–30, 2007), Romney performed best among very conservative voters who did not attend church regularly.

Among Iowa's very conservative voters, Romney faced two obstacles: Huckabee among evangelicals (which we discussed in Chapter 4), and among seculars, former Tennessee senator Fred Thompson. Thompson was a down-the-line conservative, with conservative movement positions on everything from low taxes to free trade to immigration to abortion. He had been elected to the Senate in the 1994 wave that gave Republicans control of the House for the first time since 1954, and had been an enthusiastic part of the Republican Revolution that sought to cut government. Despite being from Tennessee, Thompson was not an overtly religious man. With a consistently conservative record and a secular persona (with a prior career as a Hollywood actor to boot), many very conservative seculars found him attractive. Indeed, the secular conservative magazine *Human Events* endorsed Thompson in early 2008.

When he entered the race in fall 2007, Thompson garnered considerable attention, but his campaign failed to raise money, build organization, or gather momentum. By the time of the Iowa caucuses, Thompson was largely an afterthought, and only won 13 percent of the vote statewide. Among very conservative seculars, however, he was Romney's chief obstacle. Thompson and Romney each carried a third of these voters on caucus night; no other candidate did better than one of nine voters in this faction.

In New Hampshire and Michigan, Romney enjoyed a home-field advantage (he was born in Michigan, governed New Hampshire's southern neighbor Massachusetts, and owned a summer home in the Granite State), and Thompson's faltering campaign was nowhere to be seen. Romney finished a close second to McCain in New Hampshire, and won Michigan outright. In both cases, he significantly outperformed his statewide percentage among very conservative seculars, winning outright majorities in multicandidate fields (Figure 5.3). But Thompson bedeviled Romney one more time before he departed the race, in the key state of South Carolina. Thompson, Romney, and McCain all finished with roughly a quarter of very conservative seculars.

On January 19, the same day as South Carolina, Romney easily won the caucus in Nevada, home of a significant Mormon population. From that date until he dropped out on February 7, Romney established himself as the favorite of very conservative seculars (Table 5.3). In state after state, his performance among very conservative seculars bested his overall statewide numbers. Romney failed to lead among this faction in just two

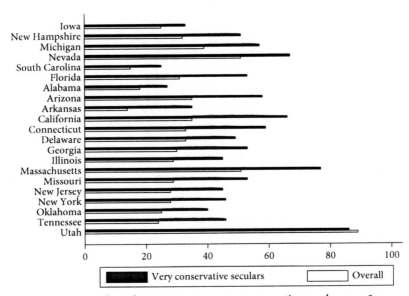

FIGURE 5.3   *Romney's performance among very conservative seculars, 2008*
Source: Weighted exit poll data, 2008.

DOI: 10.1057/9781137577535.0010

TABLE 5.3 *Candidate performance among very conservative seculars, 2008*

Primary/caucus	Date	Huckabee	McCain	Romney
Iowa (caucus)	January 3	11	9	33
New Hampshire	January 8	6	20	51
Michigan	January 15	10	16	57
South Carolina	January 19	19	27	25
Nevada (caucus)	January 19	3	6	67
Florida	January 29	7	22	53
Alabama	February 5	31	36	27
Arizona	February 5	4	26	58
Arkansas	February 5	45	10	35
California	February 5	2	25	66
Connecticut	February 5	19	20	59
Delaware	February 5	14	33	49
Georgia	February 5	29	13	53
Illinois	February 5	18	26	45
Massachusetts	February 5	2	17	77
Missouri	February 5	33	12	53
New Jersey	February 5	10	39	45
New York	February 5	17	27	46
Oklahoma	February 5	22	34	40
Tennessee	February 5	16	19	46
Utah	February 5	0	11	86
Louisiana	February 9	40	38	12*
Maryland	February 12	15	50	18*
Virginia	February 12	49	36	9*
Wisconsin	February 19	35	53	2*
Ohio	March 4	23	62	*
Texas	March 4	39	44	*
Vermont	March 4	25	55	*

* withdrew from race
Source: Weighted exit poll data, 2008.

states (Alabama) of the 17 in which exit polls were taken. He succeeded in attracting these voters far from his home territory of the Northeast, including states in the deep South such as Georgia, Oklahoma, and Tennessee.

Once Romney departed the race on February 7, very conservative seculars had a choice between McCain, the champion of moderate and liberal Republicans, and the remaining "very conservative" alternative, Mike Huckabee. In the seven contests after February 7 for which we have exit-poll data, McCain carried a plurality or majority among very conservative seculars in five, including two of the four southern states. In fact, McCain's share of the very conservative secular vote was over

DOI: 10.1057/9781137577535.0010

50 percent in Wisconsin, Ohio, and Vermont. Huckabee only defeated McCain in Louisiana and Virginia, and even here he managed only a 46-40 margin.

The 2012 nomination contest: Romney endures

In 2008, Romney enjoyed success among very conservative seculars, particularly after the field of candidates shrank and Thompson was winnowed out of the field, even though he always trailed McCain in the overall contest. Four years later, however, in a cycle in which Romney held significant campaign advantages and was often regarded as the frontrunner, very conservative secular voters were shopping for alternatives to a candidate who had created "Romneycare." In fall 2011, both Perry and Newt Gingrich had enjoyed bursts of popularity that had enabled each to eclipse Romney temporarily. A Pew Research Center national poll taken in December 2011 (Pew, December 7-11, 2011) showed that while Romney enjoyed an advantage among moderate and liberal Republican voters, he was roughly even with Gingrich and Perry among very conservative seculars. After the initial contests in Iowa (where Romney was initially, and erroneously, declared the victor) and New Hampshire, Romney was widely regarded as the frontrunner for the nomination. Yet the frontrunner struggled among this faction throughout the primaries, especially in southern states.

In the Iowa caucuses, Romney managed to carry just one of four very conservative seculars—better than he performed among all caucus goers, but only marginally. He dominated this category in New Hampshire, as he did across the board in this New England state. But in South Carolina, Romney lost very conservative seculars narrowly (40-37) to Gingrich, who won the state and briefly revived his moribund campaign. The same result occurred among this faction in Florida, where Gingrich ran even with Romney (39–38) among very conservative seculars even while losing the state overall by almost 15 percent.

After his victory in Florida, Romney was widely recognized as the presumptive frontrunner, despite losing subsequent Minnesota and Colorado caucuses to Rick Santorum. But Romney's success among very conservative seculars never extended to the South, as it did in 2008. He only led this faction in two southern states, Maryland and Virginia (in which Gingrich and Santorum failed to get on the ballot); in others, he finished as poorly as third. Romney performed well among very

DOI: 10.1057/9781137577535.0010

conservative seculars elsewhere, including Arizona and Nevada in the West (both of which have a significant Mormon presence which clearly helped Romney); and in New England, his home state of Massachusetts, as well as Vermont. In the Midwest, he achieved a narrow, (41–34) victory among this group over Santorum in Ohio, and a wider (50–33) win in Michigan.

Table 5.4 shows how Santorum's appeal to this group was always limited by his intensely religious image. In non-Southern states prior to Gingrich's fade into irrelevance after his defeats in Alabama and Mississippi, Santorum never received more than 35 percent of the very conservative secular vote. Even in the deeply evangelical South, Santorum never received more than 42 percent (Louisiana) of this faction's votes. Indeed, he lost very conservative seculars to Gingrich in Alabama and Mississippi even while he won statewide.

Gingrich's fading appeal did not boost Santorum at all among this group. While he received 42 percent in Louisiana (which is likely due to the Pelican's State's significant Catholic population, the only Southern

TABLE 5.4 *Candidate performance among very conservative seculars, 2012*

Primary/caucus	Date	Gingrich	Romney	Santorum
Iowa (caucus)	January 3	13	24	29
New Hampshire	January 10	14	46	15
South Carolina	January 21	40	37	15
Florida	January 31	39	38	17
Nevada (caucus)	February 4	21	54	11
Arizona	February 28	17	56	22
Michigan	February 28	9	50	33
Georgia	March 6	51	32	13
Massachusetts	March 6	6	74	14
Ohio	March 6	17	41	34
Oklahoma	March 6	39	13	37
Tennessee	March 6	30	24	39
Vermont	March 6	17	39	19
Virginia	March 6	*	67	*
Alabama	March 13	40	24	33
Mississippi	March 13	36	33	21
Illinois	March 20	11	45	36
Louisiana	March 24	21	33	42
Maryland	April 3	12	50	32
Wisconsin	April 3	5	52	35

* did not qualify for ballot
Source: Weighted exit poll data, 2012.

DOI: 10.1057/9781137577535.0010

state with a significant number of Santorum's co-religionists), he returned to his established 31-36 percent range of the very conservative secular vote in Illinois, Maryland, and Wisconsin. Romney's share of the very conservative secular vote rose from his previously established level, reaching 50 percent in Maryland and Wisconsin. He had previously won a majority of this group's vote in states where he had strong ties (Michigan, Massachusetts) or which had strong above-average Mormon voting shares (Nevada, Arizona). While some very conservative voters rejected him to the end, Romney rather than Santorum was the beneficiary of secular conservative voters choosing between the final two contenders. Given what we know about this group's preferences and proclivities, it would have been shocking had the result been different.

Conclusions

Conventional wisdom tells us that moderate and liberal voters in Republican presidential primaries should find themselves frustrated, marginal players in their party's nomination process. The Republican Party is, after all, America's conservative party. But in terms of results, very conservative secular voters have most cause to be disgruntled over the past decade. In 2000, 2008, and 2012, their first choices for presidential nominee have exited the contest early. As a result, the very voters who care the most about conservative values and ideology have been the ones who have to compromise their ideals and make do with second-best candidates. One key reason for this faction's frustration is the gulf between the secular and religious that exists within the Republican Party. Although both very conservative evangelicals and very conservative seculars are "values voters" who prefer candidates who are exemplars of conservatism, their conservative priorities differ significantly. In 2016, the champion of very conservative seculars will once again face the challenge of making common cause with their evangelical brethren and uniting the Right.

DOI: 10.1057/9781137577535.0010

Note

1   "Soft libertarians" are Republican voters who emphasize small government and personal liberty issues when voting, but are not so dogmatic in their beliefs or their attitude to politics to leave the GOP for the Libertarian party or refrain from voting. These voters might sound like Cato Institute scholars or *Reason* magazine editors, but they continue to express themselves primarily through Republican politics.

DOI: 10.1057/9781137577535.0010

6

The Paths to the 2016 Republican Nomination

Abstract: *In this chapter, we develop the concept of early primaries and caucuses as "knockout rounds." These first contests in the process not only bestow momentum, they also crown the champions of the various factions within the Republican Party. Rick Santorum and Mike Huckabee, for example, did not benefit from winning Iowa simply because they outperformed media expectations. They also benefited because they won Iowa by successfully courting conservative evangelicals—and thus became the national champion of that faction the day after Iowa. In similar fashion, John McCain and Mitt Romney gained from winning New Hampshire by earning the allegiance of moderate and liberal Republicans seeking a champion. After the knockout rounds, surviving candidates seek to build a coalition of voters from other factions.*

Keywords: presidential elections; presidential primaries; Republican Party

Olsen, Henry, and Dante J. Scala. *The Four Faces of the Republican Party: The Fight for the 2016 Presidential Nomination.* New York: Palgrave Macmillan, 2016. DOI: 10.1057/9781137577535.0011.

DOI: 10.1057/9781137577535.0011

Our study of the behavior of Republican presidential primary voters since 2000 offers the following insights into the battle for the 2016 GOP nomination. First, we make the case that Republican voters' ideology, combined with their level of religiosity, is a significant factor in their decisions as to who should be their nominee. Although it is true that Republican primary voters' issue positions are closer to one another than they are to Democrats, our analysis demonstrated how each of the four factions displays a distinctive set of issue priorities, as well as a distinctive set of qualities they prefer to see in their nominee. Second, we demonstrate that the first contests of the nomination cycle are most important because they determine the champions of these four factions; in other words, the early battles in places such as Iowa and New Hampshire take place within factions, and determine for the remaining Republican voters in other states the most viable candidates—this, to us, is the essence of momentum. The middle and later rounds are all about building coalitions, as voters seek the candidate who, if not an ideal fit, most closely matches their wishes.

Our analysis of the Republican electorate helps to solve a puzzle: In 2008 and again in 2012, why did the so-called conservative party nominate candidates who were the favorites of the party's moderates? The moderate faction of the GOP has gotten its way because it succeeded in unifying behind a single candidate earlier in the nomination process. In contrast, very conservative voters have again and again found themselves at odds with one another, despite their common ideology. Although very conservative evangelicals and very conservative secular voters both want a nominee who shares their values, they disagree amongst themselves as to what those values should be. This brings us to another important dividing line within the Republican Party: religiosity. Although the GOP is often depicted as the "religious party" (compared to the secular Democrats), a significant portion of Republicans is secular in its outlook. On abortion, they are either pro-choice, or at least want a candidate who will not make that issue a top priority. On the other side, very conservative evangelicals want a nominee who will make moral issues a centerpiece of their administration. Again and again, conservative elites have failed since 2000 to build a consensus behind a candidate—and as a result, somewhat conservative voters have retained the balance of power in nomination contests.

The preceding chapters have laid out the currents, eddies, and shoals that all 2016 Republican candidates will navigate to bring their

DOI: 10.1057/9781137577535.0011

nomination voyage home safely to port. This chapter brings these elements together and shows how their interaction offers different candidates different paths to a victorious journey.

Message + momentum = victory

All of a candidate's 2015 activity is essentially geared to one goal: become the first choice of one of the four factions. One ought to try to be acceptable to other factions, but if a candidate is acceptable to all but the favorite of none, that person will not make it out of the early races.

The four carve-out states (Iowa, New Hampshire, South Carolina, and Nevada) are essential to a candidate because each race favors a different one of the four factions. Victory in that state solidifies the winning candidate's hold on that faction, as the resultant burst of earned media gives that person an unparalleled chance to communicate his message without much media or opposition criticism.

In the modern (post-1968) era, no candidate stays in the race or has a serious chance to win if he has not won one of the very early-voting states.[1] Even a candidate with a "firewall" state or states in the middle stages will find that protection insufficient if he loses all of the first four contests. Rudy Giuliani discovered this to his dismay in 2008, when he abandoned his New Hampshire campaign in favor of later contests in Florida, New York, and New Jersey. On paper, this move appeared geographically and ideologically sound. Republican voters in those three states tend to be more moderate, and certainly knew of Giuliani. But even a politician as famous as "America's Mayor" became an afterthought in the wake of John McCain's comeback victory.

Once the field is winnowed, the remaining faction winners compete in the next 10–20 states to see who can establish a lead. We often find at this point that one or more of the factions has lost its champion, either because that candidate failed to win the faction by a large enough margin, or was unacceptable enough to the other factions that he failed to win a single race. Voters in these leaderless factions do not, however, pack up and go home. They instead examine the remaining candidates to find the least objectionable person.

It is here that a candidate's broad acceptability comes into play. A candidate can become the darling of one of the smaller factions, as McCain did among moderates in 2000 and Mike Huckabee did among conservative

DOI: 10.1057/9781137577535.0011

Southern evangelicals in 2008. But such overwhelming support often comes at a price: the very focus on that group's priorities that made the candidate beloved by the faction often means that the candidate has failed to stress the priorities held by those in other factions. The other factions, then, unite behind a rival faction winner who appeals most broadly even if their support is lukewarm, as much of Mitt Romney's was in the final stages of his 2012 battle with Rick Santorum.

Sometimes one candidate does so well in these middle stages that the race is over. Bob Dole accomplished this in 1996, as did George W. Bush in 2000. In other years, the middle stages narrow the race to just two candidates, who then fight each other for the nomination. These battles have occurred in 2008, when Huckabee knocked out Romney in the middle stages, and in 2012 when Rick Santorum bested Newt Gingrich. In both cases, however, the resultant one-on-one battle proved short, as Huckabee and Santorum appealed only to the social conservative wing of their party. The other three factions quickly united behind the favorite of the somewhat conservative group and a series of decisive victories (Texas and Virginia in 2008; Illinois and Wisconsin in 2012) quickly brought the race to a close.

This analysis challenges common methods of analyzing Presidential nomination contests. These methods contend that money, endorsements, and momentum have the most decisive impact on the ultimate outcome. These factors are indisputably important, but it is crucial to understand how both are ultimately subordinate to a third factor, message. Even with money or momentum, potential nominees cannot win if they do not have the right message that appeals first to one of the four factions, and then to voters in other factions when their preferred candidates drop out.

No experience better exemplifies the subordinate nature of money than that of John Connally in 1980. Connally, a former Governor of Texas and U.S. Treasury Secretary, raised $11 million, an incredible amount of money by 1980 standards. He was widely thought to be a potentially serious competitor to Ronald Reagan in large part because of his fundraising and stature. Instead, he garnered only one delegate, Ada Mills of Arkansas, and dropped out of the race after a decisive loss to Reagan in South Carolina.

Connally's defeat is not difficult to understand, once one applies the theory of factions that we advance. In 1980, the very conservative vote was united. The religious right was still in its infancy and social conservatism

DOI: 10.1057/9781137577535.0011

as a separate force within the GOP did not begin to emerge until Pat Robertson's candidacy in 1988. Reagan was clearly the head of that faction, a position of leadership he had earned through nearly sixteen years of concerted effort. Connally was no man's moderate, so any hope he had was to corner the somewhat conservative vote and use it as his base.

George H. W. Bush, however, beat him to the punch. Bush contested the Iowa caucuses while Connally campaigned in New Hampshire and South Carolina. Bush won the caucuses and rode national media momentum to national prominence, becoming the somewhat conservative faction's preferred candidate. Connally's money could not counteract the tens of millions of dollars of free, positive media that Bush's victory gave him. Connally finished a poor fifth in the Granite State, getting only 2 percent of the vote. Connally could not recover and he split the non-very conservative vote with Bush in South Carolina, allowing Reagan to deliver a 54-30 thumping that drove him from the race.

McCain's failure to win in 2000 demonstrates the subordinate nature of momentum. His massive 18-point win in New Hampshire vaulted him to national media attention and the front of the contest. Almost unnoticed in the hullabaloo, however, was that McCain owed his victory to an overwhelming margin among moderates and liberals. These voters comprised nearly half of the Granite State's voters. Moreover, George W. Bush suffered among very conservative secular voters from competition with Steve Forbes. When Forbes dropped out of the race after New Hampshire, however, these voters were left without their leader. Bush had offered a much more aggressive tax cut plan than had McCain, so when South Carolina voted, Bush's margin among very conservative voters (both religious and secular) was even larger than McCain's lead among moderates. Since moderates and very conservative voters had roughly equal strength in South Carolina, this meant the winner of the somewhat conservative bloc would win the state. Bush prevailed among this group, and went on to win somewhat conservative voters in almost every other state. After South Carolina, McCain only won in New England states whose moderate GOP electorate mirrored that of New Hampshire's, his home state of Arizona, and Michigan, where a coalition of Democrats and moderate independents and Republicans prevailed.

McCain could have won the nomination had he been wiser about how to use his momentum from New Hampshire. The day after the first-in-the-nation primary, he was still an unknown commodity to most voters outside of Arizona. He needed to campaign as the candidate of somewhat

DOI: 10.1057/9781137577535.0011

conservatives and moderates, as he had done with success in his home state. Instead, he campaigned as a fresh voice and seemed to enjoy taunting established conservative views. This infuriated the very conservative voter, and angered enough somewhat conservative voters that McCain could not win, even though he encouraged tens of thousands of non-GOP moderates to support him.

How 2016 will play out: states and factions

The carve-out states

As noted above, each of the first four states is tilted toward one of the GOP's four factions. Iowa favors very conservative religious voters; New Hampshire favors moderates and liberals; South Carolina is always won by the somewhat conservative's choice; and Nevada is most hospitable to the very conservative secular voter.

IOWA (30 delegates): Santorum's narrow win in 2012 confirmed what insiders long knew: the Iowa winner is always the very conservative

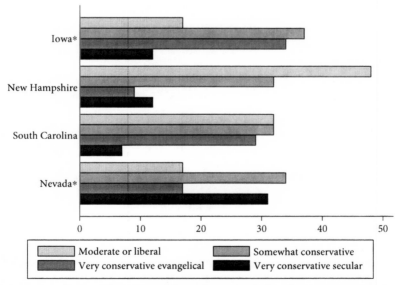

FIGURE 6.1   *Composition of Republican electorates in first four contests of 2016*
Source: Weighted exit poll data, 2008 and 2012.

DOI: 10.1057/9781137577535.0011

evangelical voter's choice. Indeed, one can hardly understate the dominance of this group. Fifty-seven percent of all 2012 Iowa GOP caucus goers were evangelicals; 47 percent said they were very conservative.[2] Santorum achieved his margins exclusively among these groups, garnering 32 percent of the total evangelical vote and 37 percent among very conservative voters who were also evangelical.

This was the third consecutive caucus win for the choice of Iowa's very conservative evangelicals, dating back to 2000. In 2008, 60 percent of caucus goers were evangelicals and 45 percent were very conservative. Huckabee garnered his support here, receiving 46 percent of the evangelical vote and 46 percent among the very conservative evangelicals.

George W. Bush also relied on very conservative evangelical support to win his race against Steve Forbes. While Bush appealed to the party's somewhat conservative center, he also won a plurality (29 percent) of the very conservative evangelical vote.

The very conservative evangelical choice could lose Iowa, but only if that faction splits evenly between two or more contenders and none of those men have much appeal outside these voters. Barring that, Iowa will propel a religiously oriented conservative into the second round of races.

NEW HAMPSHIRE (23 delegates): The national media has been slower to catch on to the Granite State's modern leanings. Anti-tax candidates were historically strong here, and it is still true that New Hampshire is one of the few states without an income tax. But no candidate who has run primarily on a low-tax platform has won, or even come close, here since the 1980s. Jack Kemp ended his 1988 bid after a disappointing 13 percent, and low-tax advocate Steve Forbes did little better in 1996 or 2000.

New Hampshire today is a bastion, perhaps the most important bastion, of moderation in the Republican nomination process. Moderates and liberals were easily the largest faction in each Republican primary since 1996, comprising between 45 and 49 percent of the total electorate. This is enhanced by New Hampshire's ballot rules that allow registered Independents to cast ballots in either party's primary. Nevertheless, it is clear that moderate Independents cast large shares of the Republican primary vote even when, as in 2000 and 2008, the Democrats also have a highly competitive primary.

When moderates are strongly behind one candidate, as they were with McCain in 2000 and 2008, their choice will prevail so long as he is not so far to the left that somewhat conservative voters reject him by large margins. When moderates are split, as they were in 1996 between Bob

DOI: 10.1057/9781137577535.0011

Dole and Lamar Alexander or in 2012 between Jon Huntsman and Ron Paul, a more conservative candidate can slip through and capture New Hampshire.

In 1996, that candidate was culture warrior Pat Buchanan. It's unlikely, however, that cultural conservatives remain as strong today as they were then. New Hampshire has one of the smallest shares of evangelicals (22 percent of Republican primary voters in 2012) of any of the major primary states. It also has a relatively tiny share of very conservative voters, ranging in the last three races between 16 and 21 percent of the electorate. Somewhat conservatives represent one-third of the electorate; should moderates divide, it is likely that somewhat conservatives' choice will prevail, as happened with Mitt Romney in 2012.

SOUTH CAROLINA (50 delegates): The Palmetto State has a very conservative reputation, and it is true that evangelical Christians make up a large share (65 percent in 2012) of the electorate. Nevertheless, the single most important group in the electorate is the somewhat conservative vote. Their choice is always South Carolina's winner.

These voters' choice must have significant support among one of the other two main blocs, moderates or very conservative evangelicals, to prevail. Moderates are surprisingly numerous in this Southern state, usually making up about 30 percent of the total electorate. Very conservative voters here tend to be more religious than secular: "economy first" conservatives such as Fred Thompson in 2008 or Mitt Romney in 2012 do much more poorly than do "religion first" candidates such as Huckabee in 2008. The most typical winning coalition is that built by Newt Gingrich in 2012 and George W. Bush in 2000, an alliance between the very conservative religious bloc and the somewhat conservative voter. But the moderate-somewhat conservative coalition has also prevailed, namely, in 2008 with John McCain's four-point victory.

NEVADA (30 delegates): Nevada's caucus usually gets the least attention of the four carve-out states, but it nevertheless can be a crucial state for a very conservative candidate who does not focus on religious and social issues to break out as a contender for the nomination. Entrance polls show that Nevada caucus goers are very conservative (49 percent in 2012; 40 percent in 2008) and not evangelical (only 28 percent of Nevada's voters were evangelicals in 2012). They are also very affluent: 28 percent made $100,000 or more in 2012, the highest share of any Republican

DOI: 10.1057/9781137577535.0011

electorate. The candidate who makes a strong, anti-government appeal, as U.S. Senate nominee Sharron Angle did in 2010, has the inside track to win Nevada's caucus. Back in 1996, Steve Forbes received more than 19 percent of the vote in the Nevada primary even though he had already dropped out. This was easily his highest share of the vote in any state following his departure from the race, suggesting a very strong intrinsic appeal for any fiscally focused, secular conservative.

These proclivities were muted in the last two races because of the state's large Mormon presence. About 25 percent of the Nevada caucus electorate was Mormon in 2008 and 2012, and they overwhelmingly supported their co-religionist, Mitt Romney. Nevada does have a larger share of Mormons in its population than most states, so it is likely that Mormons will continue to have an outsized influence on the 2016 outcome. Without Romney in the race, however, it is difficult to predict whether they will turn out as strongly. They certainly will not give any candidate 88 percent of their vote, as they gave Romney in 2012.

Historically, only candidates who have won at least one of these four states move forward with any reasonable chance of winning. While at this writing eight of the fifteen declared candidates all could theoretically count on a home-state victory by mid-March to fuel a flagging campaign, in the past such victories have only delayed an inevitable defeat for someone who has already failed in the first four contests.

How the middle campaign stage works

Most observers have a reasonable, if imprecise, grasp on the dynamics of the early contests. Where they often fall short is in understanding how the next stage of the campaign unfolds. It is here that we can see the faction theory unfold as candidates with money but limited message appeal stumble, and those with message but little cash still win in states favorable to their message.

Those seeking to understand this middle stage of the race must understand that voters without a factional favorite will look at each remaining candidate and vote for the person who has a message closest to the candidate they had preferred. This is not an absolute choice; these voters effectively vote for the "lesser of two evils" in this stage of the race. Thus, the identity of the remaining candidates, and the factions which they represent, is crucial in assessing which of the remaining candidates is likely to win majority support among each of the unled factions.

DOI: 10.1057/9781137577535.0011

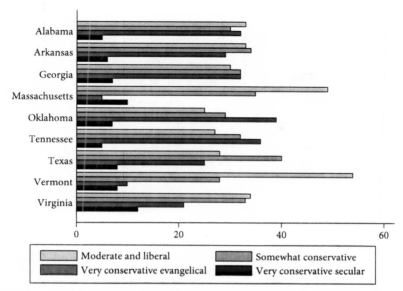

FIGURE 6.2 *Composition of Republican electorates in March 1 primaries, 2016*
Source: Weighted exit poll data, 2008 and 2012.

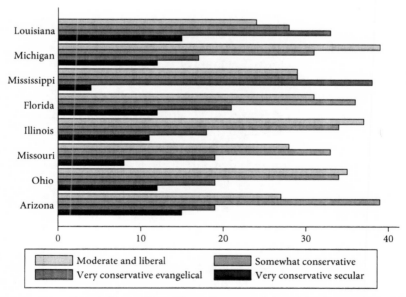

FIGURE 6.3 *Composition of Republican electorates in later March primaries, 2016*
Source: Weighted exit poll data, 2008 and 2012.

DOI: 10.1057/9781137577535.0011

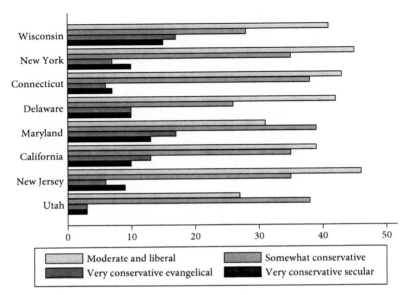

FIGURE 6.4 *Composition of Republican electorates after April 1, 2016*
Source: Weighted exit poll data, 2008 and 2012.

We can see this axiom at play in the 2008 nomination race. Three candidates split the early states: Mike Huckabee won Iowa on the strength of evangelical votes; John McCain won New Hampshire by splitting somewhat conservatives with Mitt Romney and decisively carrying moderates, and won South Carolina over Huckabee with a similar coalition; and Romney won the Nevada caucus in a landslide. Michigan voted early that year, and Romney beat McCain handily in the state of his birth with a coalition of very conservative secular voters and somewhat conservatives. Thus, while Ron Paul and Rudy Giuliani remained in the race, neither had a serious chance to win as the battle moved to Florida.

Romney had significantly more money to spend than either of his opponents, and Giuliani spent heavily in an attempt to climb back into the race. Nevertheless, McCain won the Sunshine State by five points over Romney on the back of his now steady coalition of moderates and an even share of the somewhat conservative vote. Romney's inability to win over religious conservatives doomed him here. Huckabee won only 14 percent, but he won a third of Florida's small share of religious conservatives, denying Romney crucial votes in this winner-take-all state.

DOI: 10.1057/9781137577535.0011

The race then moved to the 20 states voting on Super Tuesday. Each of the remaining candidates had their home state (or in Romney's case, his 2 home states, Utah and Massachusetts) scheduled on this day, leaving them to battle over the remaining 16. Of the three, both McCain and Romney had some momentum as each had won a big state fairly recently. Romney also had a commanding lead in money, as his ability to self-finance his race meant no one could best him on the airwaves. Huckabee was in the weakest position according to the conventional wisdom, having lost every state since his initial victory in Iowa and placing well behind the leaders in the two most recent races, Michigan and Florida.

It was nevertheless Huckabee who knocked Romney out of the race on Super Tuesday, winning his native Arkansas, Alabama, Tennessee, and Georgia and finishing a close second to McCain in Missouri and Oklahoma. In each state Huckabee carried the religious conservative vote by large margins, leaving Romney with only a share of the somewhat conservative vote and non-religiously motivated movement conservatives. Message decisively beat money in those states which Romney, who was running as the conservative alternative to McCain, desperately needed.

Nor did Romney's money advantage allow him to beat McCain in states with small shares of religious conservatives. McCain decisively beat Romney in states with large percentages of moderates (New York, Connecticut, New Jersey, Delaware, and Illinois) and won in his home state of Arizona. Most importantly, he beat Romney by seven and a half points in California, again riding large margins among moderates and a small win among somewhat conservatives to a decisive victory. Despite being the favorite of the very conservative secular faction, which had united behind him after Fred Thompson dropped out, and despite having both money and momentum, Romney's lack of a message with broad enough appeal doomed his campaign.

The overriding importance of message was aptly demonstrated in the short final phase to the race. With Romney out, his voters—primarily a mix of very conservative secular and somewhat conservative voters—had to decide which candidate to support. After Romney's exit, McCain dominated Huckabee among somewhat conservative voters in almost every remaining primary. He also led Huckabee among very conservative seculars in most contests; Huckabee's success among very conservative evangelicals did not transfer to the other branch of very conservative voters. Huckabee barely improved his standing among somewhat conservative

DOI: 10.1057/9781137577535.0011

and moderate voters even in his best state (Louisiana) and significantly gained ground on McCain only among very conservative Virginians. Even this gain, however, was more than counteracted by McCain's very significant gains among somewhat conservative voters and moderates. In short, it appears that likely Romney voters who were not very conservative overwhelmingly shifted to McCain, while those who were very conservative largely split between the two survivors.

Who will win? An analysis

These factors will again play themselves out in the 2016 battle, which in turn allows us to begin to think about alternative scenarios that are likely to develop. While it is impossible at this stage to predict a winner, it is possible to explain how a winner is likely to emerge and establish rough probabilities as to which scenario is the likeliest to occur.

The first step in this analysis is ascertaining which faction(s) each candidate is initially seeking to capture. While most candidates are competing for support among two or more factions, each also has one in which he or she has the strongest potential. Candidates will act to tie down that faction's support before they focus on the others.

Very conservative, religious: As befits a party with strong activism on the right, this is a very crowded faction. Five candidates appear as of this writing to be seriously competing for this group's favor: Huckabee, Texas Senator Ted Cruz, Louisiana Governor Bobby Jindal, former Pennsylvania Senator and 2008 Iowa caucus winner Rick Santorum, and neurologist Ben Carson. As of early October, Cruz and Carson had emerged as the strongest contenders.

This group traditionally has wanted to hear about social issues such as abortion, same sex marriage, and reversing cultural decline. It has also wanted to hear about how the candidate's faith directly affects his public life. Virtually alone among the major voting groups, religious conservatives not only are open to strong expressions of religious faith, they demand it.

All of these candidates each have good reason to appeal to this group. Huckabee is a Baptist preacher, as is Cruz's father; Carson's father was a Seventh Day Adventist minister. All three easily talk about their faith as a motivating factor in their public lives. Santorum and Jindal are Catholics, but are able to talk fluidly and devotedly about the importance of faith in

DOI: 10.1057/9781137577535.0011

their lives and in the public square. Each of these candidates also takes a clearly conservative position on litmus test social issues.

Neither national nor state polls break down self-described evangelicals among those who care most about religion and morality and those who care most about other issues. Thus, they are an unreliable guide as to this group's leanings. As of early October, billionaire real estate magnate Donald Trump narrowly led Carson among all white evangelicals, which suggests Carson led among very conservative religiously-minded evangelicals. Cruz ran third, while Huckabee's support had slumped below 5 percent. (Public Policy Polling, October 1-4, 2015).

Very conservative seculars: While this group has traditionally been the smallest of the four, there is reason to believe it will be somewhat larger this time. Primary voters who still identify themselves as "Tea Party" are likely to be motivated by tax, spending, and liberty issues. These voters share concerns, although often not rhetoric or background, with the traditional, soft libertarian voters who in the past have backed Forbes, Kemp, and Du Pont.

That's good news for Cruz, who has invested the most in winning this group's nod and threatens to unseat Kentucky Senator Rand Paul as its leader. Florida Senator Marco Rubio also has some appeal to this group, and his aggressive tax cut plan is meant to compete with the others for pre-eminence here.

These voters traditionally are moved by appeals to cut taxes significantly, reduce spending, and return power from Washington, DC to state and local governments. While Wisconsin Governor Scott Walker was in the race, he often told the story of his battle with the public sector unions to cut government spending. Cruz and Paul have each played leadership roles in attacking government spending.

The Tea Party element of this group is also strongly opposed to any degree of increased immigration or legalizing the status of currently undocumented aliens, often described as "amnesty." Trump has capitalized on this to fly to the front of the polls as of early August, his rise significantly fueled by strong support from Tea Party voters of all ideologies. Cruz and Carson remain popular among Tea Party voters, with Carson outpacing Cruz among very conservative voters of all types in national polls. (Public Policy Polling, October 1-4, 2015; Pew Research, September 22-27, 2015). Former Hewlett-Packard chief executive Carly Fiorina and Rubio have both risen in support among Tea Party voters following strong performances in a September debate at the Ronald Reagan Library in California.

Somewhat conservatives: Candidates rarely fight openly for this key faction, but it is nonetheless the most important battleground of all. Given former Florida Governor Jeb Bush's weakness among very conservative voters, this group is essential to his chances. Rubio, Carson, Fiorina, Ohio Governor John Kasich and New Jersey Governor Chris Christie are also actively competing for this group. Thus far, Trump's cross-factional appeal to an angry minority even extends to these traditionally calm voters. As of early October, Trump led in the one national poll with somewhat conservative voters broken out as a separate group. (Public Policy Polling, October 1-4, 2015). Fiorina, Rubio, and Carson vied for second, with Bush a close fifth at 11 percent. Christie's support among these voters has dropped steadily, and this is the primary reason why his chance at winning the nomination has slipped dramatically in the last year.

Moderates and liberals: No candidate is outwardly competing for these voters with the possible exception of Paul, whose efforts to show support for Internet privacy, a less aggressive foreign policy, and outreach to young people have some resonance with a substantial portion of this group. Nevertheless, before Trump's rise, Bush generally led among moderates and liberals, with Paul also doing relatively well. By early October, however, Trump had surged to a large lead among moderates as well. Carson generally ran second with about 15 percent, with Bush a close third. (Public Policy Polling, October 1-4, 2015; Pew Research, September 22-27, 2015). Christie has performed better among moderates than he has overall, but nonetheless still trailed Fiorina and Rubio. Paul's support had slumped to low single digits, and Cruz's base among these voters was nearly non-existent.

Since no candidate is yet openly campaigning for these voters, this is the group that could yet see a second-tier candidate emerge to gain pre-eminence. As of early October, this appeared to be Kasich's strategy. He has stressed the need to bring people together rather than engage in partisan bickering. His super PAC has focused its advertising campaign in moderate-heavy New Hampshire. If Kasich continues with this strategy, he has a strong chance of overtaking one or more of the current top-tier candidates and riding moderate support to an early New Hampshire victory.

DOI: 10.1057/9781137577535.0011

As of October 2015, Trump has jumped to the top of the national polls with an unusually cross-factional appeal. While most polls show his support tilting slightly to the moderate or liberal voter, he is the only candidate so far who finishes first or second among all ideological factions. (Public Policy Polling, October 1-4, 2015; Pew Research, September 22-27, 2015; USA Today/Suffolk University, September 24-28, 2015). His candidacy's future, then, rests on the answer to two questions: First, can he maintain his cross-factional appeal? Second, and more importantly, can he recruit other voters from each faction as their preferred candidates drop out of the race?

The polls currently suggest that the answer to the second question is "no." Despite his rise, Trump has some of the highest negative ratings of any candidate in the GOP race. As of October 2015, around 35-40 percent of Republican primary voters say they have an unfavorable opinion of him. More voters say they will never support Trump than any other candidate. (Quinnipiac, September 17-21, 2015). This suggests that many voters not currently supporting Trump will never consider him, and voters almost never vote for a candidate whom they view negatively.

These polls also show that Trump's favorability ratings are directly correlated with self-described ideology. Even though Trump's current support cuts across factional lines, he is viewed most favorably by Tea Partiers and very conservative voters. Polls almost uniformly show the same pattern: Trump is viewed very unfavorably by moderates, is viewed slightly favorably by somewhat conservatives, and received his strongest ratings from the very conservative factions. In a mid-September Quinnipiac poll, 15 percent of Tea Partiers said they will never back Trump. That percentage rises to 22 percent among very conservative voters, 26 percent among somewhat conservatives, and 38 percent among moderates. Three of ten white evangelicals said they would not support him, and a third of women concurred. (Quinnipac, September 17-21, 2015).

These numbers could change, but past campaign experience shows that it is difficult for a candidate to improve his favorability numbers in a contested race. Rather, as negative advertising and attacks in debates increase, so too do the negative views of a candidate who is the target of these efforts. As the current frontrunner, Trump has made himself the target all other candidates need to attack. The flamboyant real estate mogul is unlikely to weather this storm.

DOI: 10.1057/9781137577535.0011

The next step is to ascertain which states lean toward supporting candidates of a particular faction. That is relatively easy to do, since virtually every state has demonstrated a clear proclivity over the past few cycles.

Northeast (VT, ME, MA, CT, RI, NY, NJ, DC) (299 convention delegates): This is the moderate Republican heartland. Moderates are either a plurality or a majority of the electorate here, and in the middle stage of the race their candidate always prevails if he has a significant share of somewhat conservative support. Even in 2000, where George W. Bush won significant majorities among somewhat conservative voters in the middle stages, McCain was able to win in Vermont, Connecticut, Rhode Island, and Massachusetts, losing Maine only because of long-standing Bush family ties to the state. Should Jeb Bush emerge as the moderate choice, he will find these states to be his firewall should he need one.

Deep South and Midwestern Caucus (AL, MS, AR, LA, TN, KS, MN, ND) (352 delegates): This is the religious conservative heartland. Evangelical, very conservative Protestants dominate in these states and their choice always prevails in the middle stages of the race. These states have also tended to vote early in the middle stage in recent cycles, giving their favored candidate a well-needed boost in momentum.

Border South (OK, TX, GA, NC, VA, KY, WV, MO) (523 delegates): These states are finely balanced between the religious conservative and somewhat conservative factions. These states are also the heartland of the secular Tea Party movement. No candidates seeking to win the nomination with the support of either of the very conservative factions can afford to lose these states. McCain's victories in Oklahoma, Texas, Missouri, and Virginia in 2008 essentially doomed the Huckabee candidacy. If the champion of the somewhat conservative faction wins here in 2016, he will likely become the nominee.

Midwest Primary and "Border North" (MI, OH, WI, IL, PA, MD, DE, FL) (454 delegates): These states are the key battlegrounds for a candidate from the very conservative factions to capture if he wants to be the nominee. Very conservative voters have a substantial presence here (often tilted toward the religious conservatives), but the balance of power is held by the somewhat conservatives and moderates. Each state has a larger percentage of moderates than is the case nationally, but not so large a share that their votes determine the outcome. In prior elections these states have been

DOI: 10.1057/9781137577535.0011

the establishment firewall, as both Santorum and Huckabee had to drop out after failing to win any of these states. A candidate able to do what Santorum and Huckabee could not—combine somewhat conservative appeal with united support from both very conservative factions—can, however, win here in the middle stages. Such a candidate would stand the best chance in Wisconsin, Ohio, and Michigan. Florida will obviously go for one of its home state favorites, Bush or Rubio, should one of them still be in the race on March 15.

Rocky Mountain West (UT, ID, CO, MT, WY, AZ) (223 delegates): These states break roughly into two groups. First, Mormons dominate the outcome in Utah and Idaho. Second, in Arizona, Colorado, Montana, and Wyoming, a combination of very conservative, secular, soft-libertarians and somewhat conservatives vie for influence, although religious conservatives maintain a strong presence in all. A candidate with united appeal from both very conservative factions and with no obstacles to receiving Mormon allegiance will find these states quite congenial in the race's middle or later stages.

Pacific West (AK, HI, WA, OR, CA) (291 delegates): These states fall into two groups, the three continental coastal states and the two non-contiguous Pacific states. Washington, Oregon, and California all favor a somewhat conservative candidate with moderate support. Given California's large haul of 172 delegates and the fact that it awards almost all of its delegates via winner-take-all at the Congressional District level, these states can give an establishment conservative crucial backing.

Alaska and Hawaii each hold caucuses with delegates bound to respect the straw vote taken prior to the proceedings. In practice, this means any candidate will get too few delegates for these states to matter much. In 2012, each state backed Romney while giving Santorum a strong second place finish. Ron Paul finished a strong third in each, again showing that soft-libertarianism has appeal in the Pacific Republican contests. Of the two, Alaska is more hospitable for a very conservative candidate to win. Steve Forbes finished a close second there in 2000 to George W. Bush, and Huckabee had a credible second-place showing to John McCain in 2008.

Nebraska, South Dakota, New Mexico, and Indiana (134 delegates): These states have traditionally held their primaries so late that there is no reliable data with which to profile their electorates. In non-Presidential races, the three Midwestern states have very strong Tea Party and religious conservative constituencies, balanced by a large somewhat conservative faction. New Mexico tends to be friendlier to somewhat conservatives, perhaps owing to the non-trivial Hispanic share of the electorate.

Territories (AS, MP, GU, VI, PR) (53 delegates): The territories historically are controlled by the small GOP establishments there and invariably go to the somewhat conservative choice.

The order in which these states vote and the manner by which they choose to allocate delegates have substantial effects on determining the ultimate nominee. For example, voting early tends to give a candidate backed by a state's dominant faction a significant momentum boost. However, those states often must then live with the fact their delegates are split between two or more candidates, limiting their ability to determine the nominee if their preferred candidate is not favored by later-voting states.

This trade-off has been amplified by RNC-sponsored rules changes that are much more prescriptive and restrictive than in any prior nomination cycle. States that vote before March 15 must award their delegates in a proportional manner, except for the four carve-out states. Since Deep Southern states have disproportionally voted early in recent cycles, this change will make it even harder for a religious or Tea Party conservative to win the nomination than in prior years.

The rise of the so-called SEC Primary has solidified this problem. Seven Southern states[3] will vote on March 1, the earliest date permitted by RNC rules after the four carve-out states. While some of the 15 candidates will undoubtedly drop out before then, the lure of so many very conservative-leaning states will surely tempt some religious or Tea Party–backed candidates to stay in the race. While these candidates might win plurality victories in what are sure to be very crowded races, the RNC's delegate allocation rules mean the winners will not emerge with large delegate leads over the somewhat conservative or moderate choice. Moreover, the somewhat conservative and/or moderate choice will receive a non-trivial number of delegates in their worst areas. So long as the more moderate states voting later in the process award their delegates along less proportional lines—and most of them have in the past—these results are likely to be a significant boon to the establishment, moderate-conservative choice.

Religious and Tea Party-backed conservative candidates are hurt even more by the decisions of Louisiana, Kansas, North Dakota, Minnesota,

DOI: 10.1057/9781137577535.0011

and Mississippi to hold their primaries or caucuses between March 1 and 15. These states will also have to award their delegates in a proportional manner, further damaging the ability of a very conservative candidate to garner enough delegates from their base to survive defeats later in the process.

This factor alone could kill the chances of a candidate backed by very conservative voters. Every state listed in the "Midwest Primary and Border North" category save one (Michigan) has chosen to allocate its delegates by some type of winner take-all method. Delaware, Florida, and Ohio will give all delegates to the statewide winner. Maryland and Wisconsin will use a hybrid system that awards three delegates to the winner of each Congressional district, and all at-large delegates to the statewide winner. Illinois and Pennsylvania will give at-large delegates to the statewide winner and directly elect congressional district delegates. Since the ballots listing directly elected delegates in Illinois include the candidate's name to whom the delegate is bound, Illinois has an effective winner-take-all system for its congressional district delegates as well.

In contrast, the states in the categories most favorable to very conservative candidates (the Deep South and Midwest Caucus and Border South groups) do not play by winner-take-all rules. Every state in both groups allocates their delegates proportionally, except North Dakota and West Virginia – which do not bind their delegates at all. Many of these states do have provisions awarding all delegates in a state or congressional district if a candidate carries more than 50 percent of the vote – but because they vote early, the likelihood that many candidates will remain in the race almost guarantees that the winners here will emerge with small delegate leads that can be easily surmounted in the later, less conservative states.

The decisions of these states to hold their contests during the proportionality window can only be explained by a misplaced belief in the momentum theory of nominations. Should a very conservative candidate without significant appeal to somewhat conservative voters, such as Huckabee or Cruz, emerge from these early races, the establishment favorite will easily be able to overcome any delegate disadvantage in the later stage of the race.

The race is likely to break down into these three stages (states are listed in the order in which they vote).[4]

DOI: 10.1057/9781137577535.0011

- ▶ Early Stage: Iowa, New Hampshire, Nevada, South Carolina
- ▶ Middle Stage: Alabama, Alaska (caucus), Arkansas, Colorado
  (caucus), Georgia, Massachusetts, Minnesota (caucus), North
  Dakota (caucus), Oklahoma, Tennessee, Texas, Vermont,
  Virginia (March 1), Wyoming (caucus); Louisiana, Kansas
  (caucus), Kentucky (caucus), Maine (caucus) (March 5); Puerto
  Rico (March 6); Hawaii (caucus), Idaho, Michigan, Mississippi
  (March 8); Guam (caucus), Washington, D. C. (caucus) (March 12);
  Florida, North Carolina, Illinois, Missouri, Ohio (March 15)
- ▶ Late Stage: Virgin Islands (caucus) (March 19); American Samoa
  (caucus), Arizona, Utah (caucus) (March 22); Wisconsin (April 5);
  New York (April 19), Connecticut, Delaware, Maryland, Pennsylvania,
  Rhode Island (April 26); Indiana (May 3); Nebraska, West Virginia
  (May 10); Oregon (May 17); Washington (May 24); California,
  Montana, New Jersey, New Mexico, South Dakota (June 7)

Once we have grouped the candidates and the states by the factions toward which they lean, we can begin to analyze how the race will play out. Trump's candidacy throws a wrinkle into our analysis, as so far he draws from all factions of the party. The primary factor behind his rise is an outsider appeal to voters without a college degree. Thus, he could win Iowa and/or New Hampshire narrowly based on his unique demographics.

The later stages of a Trump race, however, look likely to break down along classic factional lines. Polls in October 2015 show Trump is much likelier to gain votes from the Tea Party wing of the GOP than any other faction. (Public Policy Polling, October 1-4, 2015). He also gains more votes from other very conservative voters than from somewhat conservatives. And he is very unlikely to pick up many more moderate votes: polls show he is more disliked by moderates than any of the other Republican factions.

Should Trump break through, he will likely face off against a candidate favored by the moderate wing and elements of the somewhat conservative wing. That race should break down along the lines we describe below in the hypothetical Carson v. Bush or Rubio contest in the Very Conservative v. Somewhat Conservative Scenario.

While campaigning in late 2015 will determine which candidate emerges to lead each faction, there are only four reasonable non-Trump scenarios for how the nomination process will play out.

DOI: 10.1057/9781137577535.0011

The standard scenario: religious conservative vs. somewhat conservative

Three of the last four cycles (1996, 2008, and 2012) have seen a religious conservative and a somewhat conservative candidate break out from the early and middle stages and become the final two serious contenders for the nomination. In each case, the moderates and the soft-libertarian part of the very conservative seculars swung strongly behind the somewhat conservative and swiftly dispatched the religious conservative favorite.

Should that happen again, we would see one of four candidates—Bush, Fiorina, Kasich, or Rubio—emerge to battle Huckabee, Cruz, Carson, or Santorum. Neither Huckabee nor Santorum stand much of a chance against any of these somewhat conservative favorites, as the same factional shifts we have previously seen (moderates and soft libertarians prefer the somewhat conservative to the religious conservative) are unlikely to change their pattern.

Both Huckabee and Santorum seem to recognize this and are employing a more populist economic message to reach out to blue-collar, non-evangelical voters who do not always vote in Republican primaries. These voters are numerous in the usual key battlegrounds in the border south and the Midwestern primary states. Moreover, most of these states have no party registration, permitting independents or even Democrats who find that populist message attractive to vote in Republican primaries. It is worth noting that this populist message is not the Tea Party, anti-government brand of populism. Instead, these voters tend to like entitlements and favor free enterprise, a balance that Huckabee is already trying to achieve in his messaging by emphasizing his desire to protect Social Security and Medicare from cuts. This is a risky, untried strategy that will face long odds in overcoming the historic GOP factional voting patterns.

If Cruz emerges, he is likely to have done so by also emerging as the favorite of the Tea Party wing of the very conservative seculars. This will enable him to emerge from the middle stages in a much stronger position than has traditionally been the case for a candidate backed by very conservative voters. This leads to the second scenario, which we regard as the likeliest: very conservatives vs. somewhat conservatives.

In this scenario, a candidate (probably Carson or Cruz) emerges as the early favorite of both very conservative factions in Iowa and South Carolina. That person would then carry a united conservative movement

DOI: 10.1057/9781137577535.0011

(perhaps picking up the soft-libertarian part of the very conservative seculars if Paul drops out early) into the middle stages of the race. He would face off against Bush or Rubio, although there is an outside chance either Fiorina or Kasich could emerge.

The Bush/Rubio vs. Carson/Cruz race has different dimensions depending on the identity of the winners. If Carson has emerged, he would be more likely than Cruz to prevail as he has thus far shown much more appeal to the less conservative factions. If Carson has made it through the early stage, he is also likely to have put to rest any doubts that he is sufficiently "presidential." A Carson vs. Bush or Rubio race would go on for a long time, each candidate trading victories with the other as the contest moves from state to state. Bush/Rubio would clean up in the Territories, the Northeast, Florida, and the Pacific Northwest, while Carson would win the Deep South, most of the Border South, and the Rocky Mountain states. This race would come down to California, where secular soft libertarians could be decisive, and the primary states in the Midwest and Pennsylvania.

A Cruz victory would be unlikely to go on for so long because Cruz has shown little appeal to somewhat conservative voters. If very conservative voters (both religious and secular) unite behind him, he could ride their strength to more victories in the middle stages than a purely religious conservative could, but he will likely fall short in winning enough of the border south and Midwestern primary states to prevail.

Cruz could win, however, if the race unfolds like the 2000 contest did. In this scenario, a candidate who runs explicitly to the moderate wing breaks out in Iowa and New Hampshire while Cruz breaks out on the right. These simultaneous enthusiasms would propel a very conservative Cruz versus a moderate (either Kasich or Christie) for the nomination. This is the Movement Conservative Dream Scenario and leads us to uncharted territory.

It is very difficult to forecast this scenario because for the first time in living memory, the party's largest faction would have lost its favorite early on. Where will they go? If Carson were to break out on the right, he clearly could win this showdown if his opponent were Christie as he profiles better as a soft-spoken conservative to the somewhat conservative type than would the voluble, Northeast Catholic Christie. If the candidate is Kasich, however, the result could be as drawn out as a Carson vs. Bush/Rubio contest.

DOI: 10.1057/9781137577535.0011

Should Cruz break through, however, then somewhat conservatives will be faced with a dilemma: which candidate to choose when both are difficult to support? Much of that decision will be determined by the specifics of the individual campaigns. Cruz's defiant anti-establishmentarianism will bother somewhat conservative voters. Christie would be attractive to these groups because of his more establishment bearing, but should he break out, it will likely be because he adopts a populist rhetoric that traditionally puts off somewhat conservative voters. Polls through October also show that Christie remains unpopular with somewhat conservative voters. Kasich profiles best to prevail in this scenario, but his Medicaid expansion (and especially his sanctimonious defense of it) could mean somewhat conservatives do not rally to him in large enough numbers to end the race quickly.

This contest could go either way, but it is not the strangest outcome that could emerge. That award falls to our final scenario, the Moderate Dream.

This scenario assumes that a religious conservative and a moderate break out of the early races. This would likely be some combination of Huckabee or Santorum facing Christie or Kasich, with the former winning Iowa and South Carolina and the latter winning New Hampshire and Nevada.

Here we have many factions that could be leaderless in the middle and later stages. Neither Huckabee nor Santorum excites the soft-libertarians. Tea Party and soft libertarians also dislike Kasich and loathe Christie. If the race is Huckabee versus Christie, where do they go?

The somewhat conservative voter would also be leaderless and adrift in this scenario. This person will very likely lean toward Christie or Kasich should he emerge, although without much enthusiasm. Again, Kasich would be more likely to perform better than Christie, based on October 2015 polls. But one things politics teaches is that a week is forever, and seven months is an eternity. Who knows: perhaps this scenario would upset so many party leaders that a Draft Romney movement emerges.

Conclusion

Americans are rightly proud of their democracy. That word is the combination of two ancient Greek words, *demos* and *cratia*, that mean

DOI: 10.1057/9781137577535.0011

"people" and "decide." Thanks to our democracy, it is often said that here, the people rule.

The common wisdom regarding how Presidential nominating contests unfold, however, assumes that the people do not really rule. If money decides who wins, then the people are just followers who vote for the person whose name they see most on television. If momentum decides who wins, they simply follow the name they see on news shows rather than on commercials. Neither explanation for who becomes the nominee gives the people much credit.

We believe America is still a democracy where the people truly rule. The four factions of the Republican Party each have a world view they want their candidates to adopt and a set of issue preferences they want their leaders to pursue. The Republican primary process is how voters in these factions exert their will over the men and women who seek their approval; the winner is invariably the person with the most comprehensive message acceptable to a supermajority of Republican voters. In our language, the winner is the person with the best message who appeals to at least two, and usually three, of the GOP's factions.

If money works only when it communicates a message voters find persuasive, then the people still rule. If momentum is simply the way news media rapidly spread a winning candidate's message across the country, and only those voters open to the message decide to support the candidate, then the people still rule. If message is more important than money or momentum, then truly, here the people rule.

Our book conclusively shows that Republican Party voters still rule their own party. We show how they exercise their dominance and how money and momentum always fail if the message is not sufficient. For anyone interested in the inner dynamics of GOP politics, our book provides a framework that allows one to understand and influence who becomes the party's nominee.

But more importantly, our conclusion should comfort all friends of our system of government. If the people rule even in this age of mass media and sophisticated, professional campaigning, then our system remains one that can be open to change and solve our nation's challenges. If this remains true in today's big money GOP, perhaps it remains true in the country as well.

DOI: 10.1057/9781137577535.0011

Notes

1 While Iowa, New Hampshire, and South Carolina have consistently been early-voting states since 1980, the establishment of a clearly favored "first four" is a very recent development. In previous years, for example, Arizona, Florida, Michigan, and Delaware often voted before the bulk of states scheduled their primaries. Nevertheless, it remains true that no one has become the nominee since 1980 without winning at least one of these early-voting states, and no one has become the nominee since then without winning at least one of Iowa, New Hampshire, or South Carolina.

2 These data, and similar data throughout this chapter, come from the relevant state's entrance or exit poll.

3 Alabama, Arkansas, Georgia, Oklahoma, Tennessee, Texas, and Virginia.

4 This order is taken from frontloadinghq.com. Accessed October 20, 2015.

DOI: 10.1057/9781137577535.0011

Bibliography

Abramowitz, Alan I. 1987. "Candidate Choice before the Convention." *Political Behavior* 9: 49–61.

Abramowitz, Alan I. 1989. "Viability, Electability, and Candidate Choice in a Presidential Primary Election: A Test of Competing Models." *Journal of Politics* 51: 977–992.

Abramson, Paul R., John H. Aldrich, Phil Paolino, and David Rohde. 1992. " 'Sophisticated' Voting in the 1988 Presidential Primaries." *American Political Science Review* 86: 55–69.

Adkins, Randall E., and Andrew J. Dowdle. 2000. "Break Out the Mint Juleps in New Hampshire: A Forecasting Model of the Presidential Primaries." *American Politics Quarterly.*

Adkins, Randall E., and Andrew J. Dowdle. 2001a. "Is the Exhibition Season Becoming More Important to Forecasting Presidential Nominations?" *American Politics Research* 29 (3: May): 283–288.

Adkins, Randall E., and Andrew J. Dowdle. 2001b. "How Important are Iowa and New Hampshire to Winning Post-Reform Presidential Nominations?" *Political Research Quarterly* 54 (2: June): 431–444.

Adkins, Randall E., and Andrew J. Dowdle. 2002. "The Money Primary: What Influences the Outcome of Presidential Nomination Fundraising." *Presidential Studies Quarterly* 32(2): 256–275.

Adkins, Randall E., and Andrew J. Dowdle. 2005. "Overcoming Pitfalls in Forecasting Presidential Nominations." *Presidential Studies Quarterly* 35: 646–660.

DOI: 10.1057/9781137577535.0012

Aldrich, John H. 1980a. *Before the Convention: Strategies and Choices in Presidential Nominating Campaigns.* Chicago: University of Chicago Press.

Aldrich, John H. 2009. "The Invisible Primary and Its Effects on Democratic Choice." *PS: Political Science & Politics* 42 (1: January): 33–38.

Aldrich, John H., and R. Michael Alvarez. 1994. "Issues and the Presidential Primary Voter." *Political Behavior* 16: 289–317.

Anderson, Christopher L. 2013. "Which Party Elites Choose to Lead the Nomination Process?" *Political Research Quarterly* 66: 61–76.

Barbera, Pablo. 2014. "Birds of the Same Feather Tweet Together: Bayesian Ideal Point Estimation Using Twitter Data." *Political Analysis* 23: 76–91.

Barker, David C. 2005. "Values, Frames, and Persuasion in Presidential Nomination Campaigns." *Political Behavior* 27 (Issue 4: December): 375–394.

Barker, David C., Adam B. Lawrence and Margit Tavits. 2006. "Partisanship and the Dynamics of 'Candidate Centered Politics' in American Presidential Nominations." *Electoral Studies* 25 (2006): 599–610.

Bartels, Larry M. 1988. *Presidential Primaries and the Dynamics of Public Choice.* Princeton: Princeton University Press.

Bernstein, Jonathan, and Casey B. K. Dominquez. 2003. "Candidate and Candidacies in the Expanded Party." *PS* 36 (2: April): 165–169.

Brams, Steven J. 1978a. *The Presidential Election Game.* New Haven: Yale University Press.

Cain, Bruce E., I. A. Lewis, and Douglas Rivers. 1989. "Strategy and Choice in the 1988 Presidential Primaries." *Electoral Studies* 8 (April): 23–48.

Campbell, James E. 1983. "Candidate Image Evaluations: Influence and Rationalization in Presidential Primaries." *American Politics Quarterly* 11: 293–313.

Chamberlain, Adam. 2010. "An Inside-Outsider or an Outside-Insider? The Republican Primary Campaign of Ron Paul from a Third-Party Perspective." *Politics & Policy* 38 (1: February): 97–116.

Christenson, Dino P., and Corwin D. Smidt. 2012. "Still Part of the Conversation: Iowa and New Hampshire's Say within the Invisible Primary." *Presidential Studies Quarterly* 42 (September): 597–621.

DOI: 10.1057/9781137577535.0012

Christenson, Dino P., and Corwin D. Smidt. 2014. "Following the Money: Super PACs and the 2012 Presidential Nomination." *Presidential Studies Quarterly* 44 (3: September): 410–430.

Clarke, H. D., E. Elliot, and T. H. Roback. 1991. "Domestic Issue Ideology and Activist Style: A Note on 1980 Republican Convention Delegates." *Journal of Politics* 53 (May): 519–534.

Cohen, Marty, David Karol, Hans Noel, and John Zaller. 2008. *The Party Decides: Presidential Nominations before and after Reform.* Chicago: University of Chicago Press.

Collingwood, Loren, Matt A. Barreto, and Todd Donovan. 2012. "Early Primaries, Viability and Changing Preferences for Presidential Candidates." *Presidential Studies Quarterly* 52 (2: June): 231–255.

Cook, Charlie. 2011. "It's Nobody's Turn." *The Cook Political Report,* March 6. http://cookpolitical.com/story/3100. Accessed October 20, 2015.

Costain, Anne N. 1980. "Changes in the Role of Ideology in American National Nominating Conventions and Among Party Identifiers." *Western Political Quarterly* 33: 73–86.

Daniel, Wallace L., and Meredith Holladay. 2008. "Church, State, and the Presidential Campaign of 2008." *Journal of Church and State* 50 (1: Winter): 5–22.

Denton, Robert E., Jr. 2005. "Religion and the 2004 [US] Presidential Campaign." *American Behavioral Scientist* 49 (1: September): 11–31.

DiSalvo, Daniel, and Jerome E. Copulsky. 2009. "Faith in the Primaries." *Perspectives on Political Science* 38 (2): 99–106.

Dowdle, Andrew J., Randall E Adkins, and Wayne P. Steger. 2009. "The Viability Primary: Modeling Candidate Support before the Primaries." *Political Research Quarterly* 62 (March): 77–91.

Dutwin, David. 2000. "Knowledge in the 2000 Primary Elections." *Annals of the American Academy of Political and Social Science* 572 (November): 17–25.

Farrar-Myers, Victoria A. and Richard M. Skinner. 2012. "Super PACs and the 2012 Elections." Paper prepared for the 2012 annual meeting of the American Political Science Association. August 30-September 2, New Orleans, LA.

Feigenbaum, James J., and Cameron A. Shelton. 2013. "The Vicious Cycle: Fundraising and Perceived Viability in U.S. Presidential Primaries." *The Quarterly Journal of Political Science* 8 (1): 1–40.

DOI: 10.1057/9781137577535.0012

Geer, John G. 1988. "Assessing the Representativeness of Electorates in Presidential Primaries." *American Journal of Political Science* 32: 929–945.

Gopoian, J. David. 1982. "Issue Preferences and Candidate Choice in Presidential Primaries." *American Journal of Political Science* 26: 523–546.

Grafstein, Robert. 2003. "Strategic Voting in Presidential Primaries: Problems of Explanation and Interpretation." *Political Research Quarterly* 56 (December): 513–519.

Green, John C., and James L. Guth. 1988. "The Christian Right in the Republican Party: The Case of Pat Robertson's Supporters." *Journal of Politics* 50: 150–165.

Guerrant, Daniel G., and Paul-Henri Gurian. 1996. "The Changing Impact of Viability during the Presidential Primary Season." *Social Science Journal* 33 (2): 137–147.

Gurian, Paul-Henri. 1986. "Resource Allocation Strategies in Presidential Nomination Campaigns." *American Journal of Political Science* 30: 802–821.

Gurian, Paul-Henri. 1990. "The Influence of Nomination Rules on the Financial Allocations of Presidential Candidates." *Western Political Quarterly* 43: 661–691.

Gurian, Paul-Henri. 1993a. "Candidate Behavior in Presidential Nomination Campaigns: A Dynamic Model." *Journal of Politics* 55: 115–139.

Gurian, Paul-Henri. 1993b. "Primaries versus Caucuses: Strategic Considerations of Presidential Candidates." *Social Science Quarterly* 74: 310–321.

Gurian, Paul-Henri, and Audrey A. Haynes. 1993. "Campaign Strategy in Presidential Primaries, 1976–1988." *American Journal of Political Science* 37: 335–341.

Hagen, Michael G., Richard Johnston, Kathleen Hall Jamieson, David Dutwin, and Kate Kenski. 2000. "Dynamics of the 2000 Republican Primaries." *Annals of the American Academy of Political and Social Science* 572 (November): 33–49.

Hasen, Richard L. 2009. "The Changing Nature of Campaign Financing for Presidential Primary Candidates," in *Nominating the President: Evolution and Revolution in 2008 and Beyond* (Citrin, Jack, and David Karol, editors). Lanham, MD: Rowman & Littlefield.

DOI: 10.1057/9781137577535.0012

Haynes, Audrey A., J. F. Flowers, and Paul-Henri Gurian. 2002. "Getting the Message Out: Candidate Communication Strategy during the Invisible Primary." *Political Research Quarterly* 55 (September): 633–652.

Haynes, Audrey A., Paul-Henri Gurian, Michael H. Crespin, and Christopher Zorn. 2004. "The Calculus of Concession: Media Coverage and the Dynamics of Winnowing in Presidential Nominations." *American Politics Research* 32 (3: May): 310–337.

Haynes, Audrey A., and Staci L. Rhine. 1998. "Attack Politics in Presidential Nomination Campaigns: An Examination of the Frequency and Determinants of Intermediated Negative Messages against Opponents." *Political Research Quarterly* 51 (September): 691–721.

Heaney, Michael T., Seth E. Masket, Joanne M. Miller, and Dara Z. Stolovitch. 2012. "Polarized Networks: The Organizational Affiliations of National Party Convention Delegates." *American Behavioral Scientist* 56 (12): 12654–12676.

Herrera, Richard. 1992. "The Understanding of Ideological Labels by Political Elites: A Research Note." *Western Political Quarterly* 45 (December): 1021–1035.

Hillygus, D. Sunshine, and Michael Henderson. "Political Issues and the Dynamics of Vote Choice in 2008." *Journal of Elections, Public Opinion & Parties* 20 (May).

Jennings, M. Kent. 1992. "Ideological Thinking among Mass Publics and Political Elites." *Public Opinion Quarterly* 56 (Winter): 419–441.

Kenney, Patrick J. 1993. "An Examination of How Voters Form Impressions of Candidates' Issue Positions During the Nomination Campaign." *Political Behavior* 315: 265–288.

Kenney, Patrick J., and Tom W. Rice. 1992. "A Model of Nomination Preferences." *American Politics Quarterly* 20: 267–286.

Kenney, Patrick J., and Tom W. Rice. 1994. "The Psychology of Political Momentum." *Political Research Quarterly* 47: 923–938.

Kenski, Henry C., and Kate Kenski. 2010. "Evangelical Voters in the 2008 Republican Presidential Nomination." In *Studies of Identity in the 2008 Presidential Campaign*, editor Robert E. Denton, Jr. Lexington Books.

Langenbach, Lisa, and John C. Green. 1992. "Hollow Core: Evangelical Clergy and the 1988 Robertson Campaign." *Polity* 25: 147–158.

DOI: 10.1057/9781137577535.0012

Lau, Richard R. 2013. "Correct Voting in the 2008 U.S. Presidential Nominating Elections." *Political Behavior* 35: 331–355.

Marietta, Morgan, and David C. Barker. 2007. "Values as Heuristics: Core Beliefs and Voter Sophistication in the 2000 Republican Nomination Contest." *Journal of Elections, Public Opinion and Parties* 17 (1: February): 49–78.

Marshall, Thomas R. 1984. "Issues, Personalities and Presidential Primary Voters." *Social Science Quarterly* 65: 750–760.

Mayer, William G., ed. 1996a. *In the Pursuit of the White House.* Chatham, NJ: Chatham House.

Mayer, William G. 1996b. "Forecasting Presidential Nominations." In *In the Pursuit of the White House*, ed. William G. Mayer. Chatham, NJ: Chatham House.

Mayer, William G., ed. 2000. *In the Pursuit of the White House, 2000.* Chatham, NJ: Chatham House.

Mayer, William G. 2003. "Forecasting Presidential Nominations: Or, My Model Worked Just Fine, Thank You." *PS* 36 (2: April): 153–157.

Mayer, William G. 2008. "Voting in Presidential Primaries: What We Can Learn from Three Decades of Exit Polling." In *The Making of the Presidential Candidates 2008*, ed. William G. Mayer. Lanham, MD: Rowman & Littlefield, pp. 169–203.

Mayer, William G. 2010. "Retrospective Voting in Presidential Primaries." *Presidential Studies Quarterly* 40 (Issue 4: December): 660–685.

McCann, James A. 1995. "Nomination Politics and Ideological Polarization: Assessing the Attitudinal Effects of Campaign Involvement." *Journal of Politics* 57 (February): 101–120.

McGowen, Ernest B., and Daniel J. Palazzolo. 2014. "Momentum and Media in the 2012 Republican Presidential Nomination. *Presidential Studies Quarterly* 44 (3: September): 431–446.

McKee, Seth C., and Danny Hayes. 2009. "Polls and Elections: Dixie's Kingmakers: Stability and Change in Southern Presidential Primary Electorates." *Presidential Studies Quarterly* 39 (2: June): 400–417.

Meirick, Patrick C., Gwendelyn S. Nisbett, Matthew D. Jefferson, and Michael W. Pfau. 2011. "The Influence of Tone, Target, and issue Ownership on Political Advertising Effects in Primary Versus General Elections." *Journal of Political Marketing* 10 (2): 275–296.

Monardi, Fred M. 1994. "Primary Voters as Retrospective Voters." *American Politics Quarterly* 22: 88–103.

DOI: 10.1057/9781137577535.0012

Mutz, Diana C. 1997. "Mechanisms of Momentum: Does Thinking Make It So?" *Journal of Politics* 59 (February): 104–125.

Norrander, Barbara. 1986a. "Selective Participation: Presidential Primary Voters as a Subset of General Election Voters." *American Politics Quarterly* 14: 35–53.

Norrander, Barbara. 1986b. "Correlates of Vote Choice in the 1980 Presidential Primaries." *Journal of Politics* 48: 156–167.

Norrander, Barbara. 1989. "Ideological Representativeness of Presidential Primary Voters." *American Journal of Political Science* 33: 570–587.

Norrander, Barbara. 1993. "Nomination Choices: Caucus and Primary Outcomes, 1976–1988." *American Journal of Political Science* 37: 343–364.

Norrander, Barbara. 2000. "The End Game in Post-Reform Presidential Nominations." *Journal of Politics* 62 (November): 999–1013.

Norrander, Barbara. 2006. "The Attrition Game: Initial Resources, Initial Contests and the Exit of Candidates During the US Presidential Primary Season." *British Journal of Political Science* 36 (July): 487–507.

Oldfield, Duane M. 1996a. "The Christian Right in the Presidential Nominating Process." In *In the Pursuit of the White House*, ed. William G. Mayer. Chatham, NJ: Chatham House.

Oldfield, Duane M. 1996b. *The Right and the Righteous: The Christian Right Confronts the Republican Party*. Lanham, MD: Rowman and Littlefield.

Olsen, Henry. 2014. "The Four Faces of the Republican Party." *The National Interest* (March–April).

Paolino, Phillip, and Daron R. Shaw. 2001. "Lifting the Hood on the Straight-Talk Express: Examining the McCain Phenomenon." *American Politics Research* 29 (September): 483–506.

Pastor, Gregory S., Walter J. Stone, and Ronald B. Rapoport. 1999. "Candidate-Centered Sources of Party Change: The Case of Pat Robertson, 1988." *Journal of Politics* 61(May): 423–444.

Paulson, Arthur. 2009. "Party Change and the Shifting Dynamics in Presidential Nominations: The Lessons of 2008." *Polity* 41 (3): 312–330.

Petrocik, John R., and Dwaine Marvick. 1983. "Explaining Party Elite Transformation: Institutional Changes and Insurgent Politics." *Western Political Quarterly* 36 (September): 345–363.

Popkin, Samuel L. 1994. *The Reasoning Voter: Communication and Persuasion in Presidential Campaigns*. Chicago: University of Chicago Press.

DOI: 10.1057/9781137577535.0012

Putnam, Josh. 2015. "FrontloadingHQ" website. http://frontloading. blogspot.com/. Accessed October 20, 2015.

Rae, Nicol C. 1998. "Party Factionalism, 1946–1996," in *Partisan Approaches to Postwar American Politics* (Byron E. Shafer, ed.), p. 41–74.

Redlawsk, David P. 2004. "What Voters Do: Information Search During Election Campaigns." *Political Psychology* 25 (4: August): 595–610.

Redlawsk, David P., Caroline J. Tolbert, and Todd Donovan. 2011. *Why Iowa? How Caucuses and Sequential Elections Improve the Presidential Nominating Process.* Chicago: University of Chicago Press.

Reiter, Howard L. 2004. "Factional Persistence with Parties in the United States." *Party Politics* 10 (3: May): 251–271.

Ridout, Travis N., and Jenny L. Holland. 2010. "Candidate Strategies in the Presidential Nomination Campaign." *Presidential Studies Quarterly* 40: 611–630.

Ridout, Travis N., Brandon Rottinghaus and Nathan Hosey. 2009. "Following the Rules?: Candidate Strategy in Presidential Primaries." *Social Science Quarterly* 90: 777–795.

Scala, Dante and Andrew Smith. 2008. "Does the Tail Wag the Dog: Early Presidential Nomination Polling in New Hampshire and the U. S." *American Review of Politics,* Fall and Winter 2007–2008, p. 401–424.

Sebold, Karen, Scott Limbocker, Andrew Dowdle, and Patrick Stewart. 2012. "The Political Geography of Campaign Finance: Contributions to 2008 Republican Presidential Candidates." *PS: Political Science & Politics* 45 (4: October): 688–693.

Sides, John and Lynn Vavreck. 2013. *The Gamble: Choice and Chance in the 2012 Presidential Election.* Princeton: Princeton University Press.

Steger, Wayne P. 2008a. "Forecasting the Presidential Primary Vote: Viability, Ideology and Momentum." *International Journal of Forecasting* 24 (2: April–June): 193–208.

Steger, Wayne P. 2008b. "Inter-Party Differences in Elite Support for Presidential Nomination Candidates." *American Politics Research* 36: 724–749.

Steger, Wayne. 2013. "Two Paradigms of Presidential Nominations." *Presidential Studies Quarterly* 43: 377–387.

Steger, Wayne P., Andrew J. Dowdle, and Randall E. Adkins. 2004. "The New Hampshire Effect in Presidential Nominations." *Political Research Quarterly* 57 (3): 375–390.

Steger, Wayne P., John Hickman, and Ken Yohn. 2002. "Candidate Competition and Attrition in Presidential Primaries, 1912–2000." *American Politics Research* 30 (5: September): 528–554.

DOI: 10.1057/9781137577535.0012

Stone, Walter J. and Alan I. Abramowitz. 1983. "Winning May Not Be Everything, But It's More than We Thought: Presidential Party Activists in 1980." *American Political Science Review* 77 (4: December), 945–956.

Wattier, Mark J. 1983a. "Ideological Voting in 1980 Republican Presidential Primaries." *Journal of Politics* 45: 1016–1026.

Weakliem, David L. 2001. "A New Populism? The Case of Patrick Buchanan." *Electoral Studies* 20 (3: September): 447–461.

Wichowsky, Amber, and Sarah E. Niebler. 2010. "Narrow Victories and Hard Games: Revisiting the Primary Divisiveness Hypothesis." *American Politics Research* 38: 1052–1071.

Wilcox, Clyde. 1992a. *God's Warriors: The Christian Right in 20th Century America*. Baltimore: The Johns Hopkins University Press.

Wilcox, Clyde. 1992b. "Religion and the Preacher Vote in the South: Sources of Support for Jackson and Robertson in Southern Primaries." *Sociological Analysis* 53: 323–331.

Wilcox, Clyde. 2002. "Wither the Christian Right: the Elections and Beyond." In *The Election of the Century and What It Tells Us about the Future of American Politics*, ed. Stephen J. Wayne and Clyde Wilcox. Armonk: M.E. Sharpe, pp. 107–124.

SURVEY DATA

The authors used polling data from the following sources for their analysis:

Gallup

National Election Pool (2008 exit polls, conducted by Edison/Mitofsky; 2012 exit polls, conducted by Edison Media Research)

NBC News / Wall Street Journal

Pew Foundation

Public Policy Polling

Quinnipiac University Poll

Suffolk University Political Research Center

Voter News Service (2000 exit polls)

Datasets from all exit polls, and several Gallup and Pew polls, were accessed via the Roper Center for Public Opinion Research, RoperExpress [distributor], Storrs, CT. Information from other polls was publicly accessible.

DOI: 10.1057/9781137577535.0012

Index

abortion, 6, 89, 123, 134
  moderates and liberals, 34,
    38, 40, 41, 47, 58
  somewhat conservatives,
    64, 65
  very conservative
    evangelicals, 81, 83
  very conservative seculars,
    108, 109
Adelson, Sheldon, 17
Alexander, Lamar, 4, 37, 42,
    58*n*1, 68, 129
Angle, Sharron, 130
attrition, primary and caucus
    voters, 12–14

Bachmann, Michele, 74
Bauer, Gary, 87, 88, 103*n*3
Bipartisan Campaign Reform
    Act (2002), 15
Boehner, John, 62
Border South, Republican 2016
    nomination, 138
Buchanan, Pat, 5–6, 9, 10, 13,
    61, 81, 103*n*3, 111, 129
Bush, George H. W., 23, 25, 126
Bush, George W., 3, 15, 19, 28,
    125–6, 128, 139
  as candidate, 87–8
  moderates and liberals, 42, 44
  nomination contest (2000),
    67–70, 88–90, 111–13
  performance among
    moderates and liberals
    (2000), 44

  performance among
    somewhat conservative
    (2000), 68, 69
  performance among very
    conservative evangelicals
    (2000), 91, 92
  performance among very
    conservative seculars
    (2000), 114
  somewhat conservatives, 61,
    65, 67–70, 138
  South Carolina, 105, 129
  very conservative
    evangelicals, 91, 92, 95, 102
  very conservative seculars,
    109
  vote in 2000, post-South
    Carolina, 91
Bush, Jeb, 17, 136, 138, 139, 142,
    143–4

Cain, Herman, 6, 105
campaign financing, super
    PACs, 16–17, 136
candidate qualities
  moderates and liberals, 38,
    39
  somewhat conservatives,
    64, 66
  very conservative
    evangelicals, 83, 86–8
  very conservative seculars,
    108, 110
Carson, Ben, 134–6, 142–4
Carter, Jimmy, 9

carve out states, 12
Casey, Bob, 97
Cheney, Dick, 3
Christie, Chris, 136, 144, 145
Clinton, Bill, 15, 41, 65, 109
Connally, John, 10, 125–6
conservatism, 112
    American, 5, 61
    Bush vote in 2000, post–South
        Carolina, 91
    Gingrich primary vote in 2012, post-
        Florida, 101
    Huckabee vote in 2008, post-South
        Carolina, 97
    McCain's vote in 2000, post-South
        Carolina, 45
    McCain's vote in 2008, post-South
        Carolina, 53
    Republican Party, 24, 106, 119
    Romney's vote in 2012, post-Florida,
        57
    Santorum primary vote in 2012,
        post-Florida, 102
    social, 6, 49, 82, 97, 125
    Tea Party, 39
Cruz, Ted, 134–6, 141, 143–5
culture warrior, 5, 61, 129

Deep South and Midwestern
    Caucus,Republican 2016
    nomination, 138, 141, 144
Defense of Marriage Act (1996), 89
Dole, Bob, 4–5, 9, 27, 37, 42, 58*n*1, 61,
    111, 125, 128–9
Dole, Elizabeth, 42, 68
DuPont, Pete, 6, 105, 135
Dutch Reformed Church, 103*n*3

elite influence,presidential
    nominations, 14–20
evangelicals, *see* very conservative
    evangelicals
exit polls, 30–2, 156

Falwell, Jerry, 89
Family Research Council, 88

FEC (Federal Election Commission),
    16
Fiorina, Carly, 17, 135–6, 143–4
Forbes, Steve, 6, 32*n*1, 130, 135, 139
    performance among moderates and
        liberals (2000), 44
    performance among somewhat
        conservatives (2000), 69
    performance among very
        conservative evangelicals (2000),
        91
    performance among very
        conservative seculars (2000), 114
    somewhat conservatives, 69
    very conservative evangelicals,
        88–90, 128
    very conservative seculars, 6–7, 105,
        109, 111–15, 126
Ford, Gerald, 9, 27
friction, nomination process,
    29–30

Gallup, 30, 46–7, 49, 156
Gingrich, Newt, 4, 6, 16–17, 125, 129
    moderates and liberals, 37, 56, 57
    performance among moderates and
        liberals (2012), 56
    performance among somewhat
        conservatives, 77
    performance among very
        conservative evangelicals (2012),
        100
    performance among very
        conservative seculars (2012), 119
    primary vote in 2012 post-Florida,
        101
    somewhat conservatives, 75–8
    very conservative evangelicals,
        98–102
    very conservative seculars, 105,
        118–20
Giuliani, Rudy, 10, 17, 46–50, 70–1, 73,
    124, 132
Goldwater, Barry, 25, 95
Graham, Billy, 88
Gramm, Phil, 6, 105

DOI: 10.1057/9781137577535.0013

Hadley, Arthur, 14
Hart, Gary, 9
Huckabee, Mike, 5, 12, 46–50, 53, 70–3,
    81–2, 101, 124–5, 141, 143, 145
  border South delegates, 138–9
  evangelical faction in 2008, 93–6
  Iowa, 10, 103n3, 128, 132–3
  performance among moderates and
    liberals (2008), 52
  performance among somewhat
    conservatives (2008), 72
  performance among very
    conservative evangelicals (2008),
    94, 96
  performance among very
    conservative seculars (2008), 117
  preference for Republican
    nomination (2007), 47
  very conservative evangelicals, 5,
    87–8, 91, 93, 134–5
  very conservative seculars, 115, 117
  vote in 2008, post-South Carolina,
    97
Huntsman, Jon, 4, 37, 54–5, 74–5, 129

ideology, 2, 20
  guiding voters, 25–6
  presidential primary voters,
    22–5
  Republican voters, 123–4
  Tea Party voters, 135
  Trump, 137
invisible primary, 9, 14–19, 46, 68
Iowa, 12–14, 59n5
  carve-out state, 124
  early voting, 147n1
  Republican composition of 2016,
    127–8
  swing voters, 103n3
  very conservative evangelicals, 92–3
issue priorities
  moderates and liberals, 41
  somewhat conservatives, 65–6
  very conservative evangelicals, 83,
    85–6
  very conservative seculars, 108, 109

Jackson, Jesse, 13
Jindal, Bobby, 134

Kasich, John, 136, 143, 144, 145
Kemp, Jack, 6, 32n1, 105, 128, 135
Kennedy, John F., 92
Kerry, John, 15
Keyes, Alan, 13, 87, 88–9, 112–13
  performance among moderates and
    liberals (2000), 44
  performance among somewhat
    conservatives (2000), 69
  performance among very
    conservative evangelicals (2000),
    90
  performance among very
    conservative seculars (2000), 114
knockout rounds, 7–8, 69, 105, 122,
    125, 133

liberals, *see* moderates and liberals
libertarianism, 58–9n3, 121n1, 139,
    143–4

McCain, John, 4–8, 5, 12, 15, 19, 25, 28,
    124, 126–9, 132–4, 138–9
  moderate maverick, 42–5, 46–52
  moderates and liberals, 37, 42–55
  nomination contest (2000), 42–5
  nomination contest (2008), 46–52,
    70–3
  nomination contest (2012), 52–8
  performance among moderates and
    liberals (2000), 43, 44
  performance among moderates and
    liberals (2008), 51, 52
  performance among somewhat
    conservatives (2000), 69
  performance among somewhat
    conservatives (2008), 71, 72
  performance among very
    conservative evangelicals (2000),
    90
  performance among very
    conservative evangelicals (2008),
    94

McCain, John – *continued*
  performance among very
    conservative seculars (2000), 114
  performance among very
    conservative seculars (2008), 117
  preference for Republican
    nomination (2007), 47
  somewhat conservatives, 61, 65,
    68–73
  very conservative evangelicals, 81–2,
    87–91, 93–5, 97
  very conservative seculars, 105,
    113–18
  vote analysis in 2000, post-South
    Carolina, 45
  vote analysis in 2008, post-South
    Carolina, 53
McGovern, George, 9
Mansfield, Harvey, 113
Mapplethorpe, Robert, 112
Mayer, William, 14–15
Medicare, 82, 143
Midwest Primary and Border North,
    Republican 2016 nomination,
    138–9, 141
moderates and liberals, 3–4
  candidate performance in 2000, 44
  candidate performance in 2008, 52
  candidate qualities, 39
  composition of electorates after
    April 2016, 132
  composition of electorates in March
    2016, 131
  finding a champion, 41–58
  issue priorities, 41
  McCain and Romney in 2012
    nomination, 52–8
  McCain in 2000 nomination, 42–5
  McCain in 2008 nomination, 46–52
  party identification, 38–9
  preferences and priorities, 37, 38
  presence in Republican primaries,
    34–7
  profile, 38
  Republican 2016 nomination, 136–8
  secularism of, 40

momentum model, primary and
    caucus voters, 10–12
Mondale, Walter, 9
Mormons
  Nevada voters, 109, 116, 120, 130
  Rocky Mountain West, 139
  Romney, 50, 55, 71, 78, 92, 93
Muskie, Ed, 9

NAFTA (North American Free Trade
    Agreement), 6, 81
Nebraska, South Dakota, New Mexico
    and Indiana, Republican 2016
    nomination, 139–40
Nevada, 12
  carve-out state, 124
  Mormon voters, 109, 116, 120, 130
  Republican composition of 2016, 127,
    129–30
New Hampshire, 12–14, 59n5
  carve-out state, 124
  early voting, 147n1
  Republican composition of 2016, 127,
    128–9
  very conservative evangelicals, 92–3
Norquist, Grover, 115
Northeast, Republican 2016
    nomination, 138

Obama, Barack, 15, 28, 39, 54–5, 66,
    74–5, 87, 111

Pacific West, Republican 2016
    nomination, 139
party identification
  moderates and liberals, 38–9
  somewhat conservatives, 64, 67
  very conservative evangelicals, 82, 83
  very conservative seculars, 107, 108
Paul, Rand, 135–6
Paul, Ron, 4, 99, 129, 132, 139
  moderates and liberals, 37, 49–50, 54,
    56, 58–9n3, 59n5
  somewhat conservatives, 74, 77, 78
Pawlenty, Tim, 74
Perry, Rick, 6, 75–6, 105, 118

Pew Foundation, 30, 118, 135–7, 156
political science, presidential
    primaries, 8–10
presidential candidates
    bringing factions in, 20–2
    faction and friction, 29–30
    personal characteristics of, 26
    priorities, 26–7
    values as guides for voters, 27–8
    viability, 28–9
presidential elections, 10, 14, 18
presidential primaries
    2016, 7–8
    candidate values as guides for, 27–8
    elite influence, 14–20
    exit polls, 30–2
    ideology and voters, 22–5
    ideology guiding voters, 25–6
    methodology, 30–2
    political science of, 8–10
    voter priorities, 26–7
primary and caucus voters
    attrition, 12–14
    momentum model, 10–12

Quayle, Dan, 67–8
Quinnipiac University poll, 137, 156

Reagan, Ronald, 9, 22–5, 27, 32n1, 88,
    95, 105, 112, 125–6, 136
Red White and Blue Fund, 17
religiosity, very conservative
    evangelicals, 85
Religious Right, 32n1, 40, 44–5, 63, 65,
    73, 84–5, 89–90, 92, 107, 112, 125
Republican Party, 4, 6, 19, 32n1, 51, 53,
    56, 78
    conservatism, 24, 49
    culture war, 28
    factions of, 2, 20–2, 146
    moderates and liberals, 34, 35, 37,
        38–9, 40
    nomination process, 9, 12
    religiosity, 123
    "Religious Right", 44
    secularism, 63

somewhat conservatives, 61
very conservative evangelicals, 82,
    86–7
very conservative seculars, 106, 119
Republican presidential 2016
    nomination, 123–4, 142
    analysis for winner, 134–42
    carve-out states, 127–30
    establishment vs. insurgents, 2
    Iowa, 127–8
    message + momentum = victory,
        124–7
    middle campaign stage, 130–4
    Nevada, 127, 129–30
    New Hampshire, 127, 128–9
    religious conservative vs. somewhat
        conservative, 143–5
    South Carolina, 127, 129
Republican primaries
    moderates and liberals in, 34–7
    somewhat conservatives, 62, 63
    very conservative evangelicals in,
        84–5
    very conservative seculars in,
        106–7
Republicans factions
    composition of electorates after
        April 2016, 132
    moderates and liberals, 3–4
    somewhat conservatives, 4–5
    very conservative evangelicals, 5–6
    very conservative seculars, 6–7
Restore Our Future, 16–17
Robertson, Pat, 4, 5, 13, 37, 42, 81, 89,
    92, 126
Rockefeller, Nelson, 25
Rocky Mountain West,Republican
    2016 nomination, 139
Romney, Mitt, 4–8, 13–17, 19, 61, 125,
    129–30, 132–4, 139
    campaign spending, 32n2
    Draft Romney movement, 145
    moderates and liberals, 37, 48–52
    Mormon religion, 50, 55, 71, 78, 92,
        93
    nomination contest (2008), 113–18

Romney, Mitt – *continued*
nomination contest (2012), 52–8,
74–8, 118–19
performance among moderates and
liberals (2008), 52
performance among moderates and
liberals (2012), 55, 56
performance among somewhat
conservatives (2008), 72
performance among very
conservative evangelicals (2008),
94
performance among very
conservative evangelicals (2012),
100
performance among very conservative
seculars (2008), 116, 117
performance among very
conservative seculars (2012), 119
preference for Republican
nomination (2007), 47
somewhat conservatives, 61, 70–8
very conservative evangelicals, 81,
88, 90–1, 93–5, 97–102
very conservative seculars, 105,
115–20
voters in 2012, post-Florida, 57
Roper Center for Public Opinion
Research, 30, 156
Rubio, Marco, 135–6, 139, 142–4

Santorum, Rick, 4–7, 12–13, 17, 37, 76,
78, 81–2, 103*n*3, 105, 125, 139, 143,
145
Iowa, 127–8, 134
Iowa caucus, 103*n*3
Minnesota and Colorado caucuses,
118
nomination contest (2012), 96–102
performance among moderates and
liberals (2012), 56
performance among somewhat
conservatives (2012), 77
performance among very
conservative evangelicals (2012),
98, 100

performance among very
conservative seculars (2012), 119
primary vote in 2012 post-Florida,
102
SEC Primary, Republican 2016
nomination, 140
secularism, 4, 40, 41, 58, 63–4, 110
seculars, *see* very conservative seculars
Social Security, 41, 65, 82, 105, 143
soft libertarians, 121*n*1, 143–4
somewhat conservatives, 4–5, 60, 61–2
abortion, 65
between secular and religious voters,
63–4
Bush dominating 2000 nomination
contest, 67–70
candidate qualities, 66
composition of electorates after
April 2016, 132
composition of electorates in March
2016, 131
issue priorities, 65–6
McCain in 2008 nomination contest,
70–3
party identification, 67
presence in primary electorate, 62,
63
profile, 64
religious conservative vs., in 2016
nomination, 143–5
Republican 2016 nomination, 136
Romney in 2012 nomination contest,
74–8
South Carolina, 12
carve-out state, 124
early voting, 147*n*1
Republican composition of 2016,
127, 129
Steger, Wayne, 19
super PAC, 16–17, 136

Tea Party, 2
conservative candidates backed by,
141–2
movement, 67, 74–5, 82, 138
somewhat conservatives, 64

undocumented aliens, 135
very conservative evangelicals, 82,
  83, 85
very conservative seculars, 108–9
territories, Republican 2016
  nomination, 140
Thompson, Fred, 6, 46–9, 70–1, 73, 93,
  105, 115–16, 118, 129, 133
Trump, Donald, 135–7, 142

very conservative evangelicals, 5–6,
  81–2
  Bush in nomination contest (2000),
    88–90
  candidate qualities, 83, 86–8
  composition of electorates after
    April 2016, 132
  composition of electorates in March
    2016, 131
  exit pollsters, 103*n*1
  Huckabee faction in 2008, 93–6
  Iowa and New Hampshire, 92–3
  nomination contest (2008), 90–2
  party identification, 82, 83
  preferences and priorities, 85–6
  presence in Republican primaries,
    84–5

profile, 82, 83
religiosity, 85
Republican 2016 nomination, 134–5
Santorum in nomination contest
  (2012), 96–102
very conservative seculars, 6–7, 105
  abortion, 108, 110
  candidate qualities, 108, 110–11
  composition of electorates after
    April 2016, 132
  composition of electorates in March
    2016, 131
  issue priorities, 108, 109–10
  nomination contest (2000), 111–14
  party identification, 107, 108
  presence in Republican primaries,
    106–7
  profile, 105–6, 108
  Republican 2016 nomination, 135–6
  Romney and nomination contest
    (2008), 113–18
  Romney and nomination contest
    (2012), 118–20
  Tea Party, 108–9
  values voters, 120

Walker, Scott, 135

DOI: 10.1057/9781137577535.0013

CPSIA information can be obtained at www.ICGtesting.com
Printed in the USA
LVOW07*1752250116

472166LV00001B/1/P